Mhòr and More

Hill Walks in Uist

◈

MARTIN MARGULIES

Published in 2011 by The Islands Book Trust

www.theislandsbooktrust.com

ISBN: 978-1-907443-12-1

Text © Martin Margulies

British Library Cataloguing in Publication Data. A CIP record for
this book can be obtained from the British Library.

Front cover image © Allan MacDonald
Image of North Aineort public footpath under snow,
winter 2011 © Beth Zeldes Margulies
Back cover and all other images © Martin Margulies

Typeset by Erica Schwarz
Printed by Martins the Printers, Berwick upon Tweed
Cover design by Jim Hutcheson

The Islands Book Trust, Ravenspoint Centre, Kershader,
South Lochs, Isle of Lewis, HS2 9QA. Tel: 01851 880737

The European Agricultural Fund
for Rural Development:
Europe investing in rural areas

**The Scottish
Government**
Riaghaltas na h-Alba

**H I E
Innse Gall**
Outer Hebrides

Dedication

This book is dedicated to Beth, Max and Adam, of course; to J.J., Isabel and Ben; to Murdo and Panda (and to the memories of Lucky, Dileas and Corrie); to my many other friends on the islands, too numerous to name, whose kindness and hospitality have meant so much to me; and to the Coast Guard helicopter crew – Lenny, Donald and the rest – who taught me a remembered lesson when they winched me off the back of Meall Mhòr.

It is dedicated also to my late father-in-law, Dr. Benjamin Zeldes. Sadly, he never did get to go fishing off Gleann Corodail.

About the author

Martin Margulies is a mostly-retired law teacher and civil rights lawyer from Connecticut, U.S.A., where he also coaches tennis. He and his wife Beth own a holiday house, on South Uist, which they and their two grown sons visit as often as possible. Martin has written two other books, 'The Early Life of Sean O'Casey' and 'The Battle of Prestonpans 1745.' He is listed in 'Best Lawyers in America.'

Note: The photographs in articles 1–38 were taken by the author using a disposable camera, with the aim of illustrating his experience of the walks, rather than to provide high-quality landscape shots.

THE ISLANDS BOOK TRUST – high quality books on island themes in English and Gaelic

Based in Lewis, the Islands Book Trust are a charity committed to furthering understanding and appreciation of the history of Scottish islands in their wider Celtic and Nordic context. We do this through publishing books, organising talks and conferences, visits , radio broadcasts, research and education on island themes. For details of membership of the Book Trust, which will keep you in touch with all our publications and other activities, see www.theislandsbooktrust.com or phone 01851 880737.

The Islands Book Trust, Ravenspoint, Kershader, South Lochs, Isle of Lewis, HS2 9QA (01851 880737)

Contents

CONTENTS

Acknowledgements

I thank Alasdair MacEachen and John Randall of the Islands Book Trust for editorial oversight and guidance, and for believing in this book. I thank Archie MacKay of *Am Pàipear* for the same. I thank Archie also for welcoming and publishing my monthly newspaper columns, and for rendering them into book format. I thank Alasdair's remarkably talented teenaged nephew, Allan MacDonald, for the beautiful cover photograph and for technical help with the other photos.

I have joked that since locals never visit the places I write about, I can invent details as I please. But locals do visit them, of course – not only visit them but often know more about them than I do. Many of these locals have shared their time and knowledge generously. Alasdair brought me to St. Kilda, the Monachs, Wiay and Sunamul. John Joseph MacDonald took me by boat to Glen Corodale, Kyle Stuley and (with his wife Isabel) the bays of Mile-Feala and Usinish; he also imparted valuable information about other remote areas. Mike Mason ferried me to Hartavagh Bay and told me about Coire na Cuilc and the bothy at Usinish. Eric and Jane Twelves introduced me to the Eaval footpath and the Drimsdale route to Hecla; they also gave me useful pointers on climbing Sheaval. John Hart showed me new ways up Beinn Mhòr. (I sometimes refer to these places by other spellings – Gaelic, Gaelicised or English – in my columns.) I thank all of these kind people. None of them is responsible for my errors.

Finally, Mike Mason and George MacLellan, experienced hill-walkers themselves (I first met Mike on top of Beinn Mhòr), encouraged me to roll the columns into a book. I forget which of us thought of it initially, but I know that their encouragement emboldened me to approach Archie, who it turned out had thought of it also. I hope that Mike, George, Archie and the others whom I've thanked here will be pleased with the result.

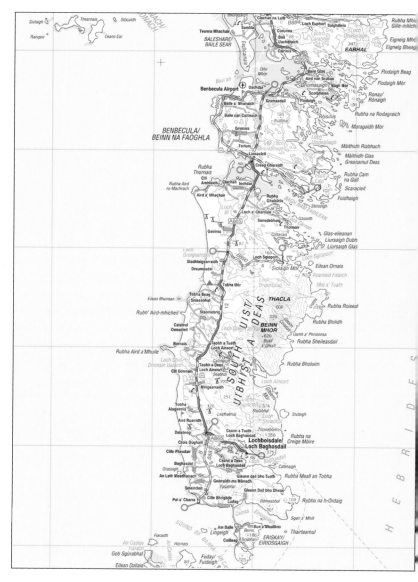

General location map.
(Reproduced by permission of Ordnance Survey on behalf of HMSO.
© Crown copyright 2011. All Rights reserved. Ordnance Survey
Licence number 100050414.)

Introduction

I first came to South Uist in October, 1987. My wife, pregnant at the time, stayed home in Connecticut. On the last afternoon of my visit, I tried to scale Beinn Mhòr, tallest of the island's peaks, but turned back about halfway up. It was a wise decision, for the light was fading, I was under-dressed, and I had no knowledge of the terrain. If I'd persisted, my hosts at the Borrodale Hotel might have had to summon a helicopter to airlift me out.

My latest visit took place this past summer. I lodged, not at the Borrodale, but in the holiday home that my wife and I had built on North Loch Aineort in 2004. And the child whom my wife was carrying during my first visit, now a strapping lad of 22, accompanied me up Beinn Mhòr with his girlfriend.

During those intervening 23 years, I have been to South Uist many times, both before and after building the holiday home, and have climbed all of the major hills, there and on the adjacent islands, from Eabhal on North Uist through to Eriskay's Beinn Sciathan. That includes multiple successful ventures up Mhòr. I've had my share of mishaps. I took one nasty spill which, interacting with a pre-existing disc condition, has cost me the partial use of my left arm, and on another occasion – which the locals have not let me forget, and which I would not forget in any event – I met up with the helicopter after all, when I became lost behind

Meall Mhòr on the North Loch Aineort coast. (At least, I now know it to have been behind Meall Mhòr; had I known it then I would not have needed the helicopter.) But for every untoward experience, I have spent dozens of glorious days exploring remote hills and glens and savouring their isolation and beauty. I am certain that mortal eyes have not beheld finer vistas since Adam and Eve bade farewell to Eden.

I've had one disappointment: I've not been able to coax my wife into joining me on my longer walks. I hold forth to her about their many benefits: the scenery, the solitude, the exercise – a hikers' magazine describes the terrain as among 'the roughest in Britain' – and the sense of accomplishment. She remains unmoved: hill-walking, to her, is merely a slog. But even she enjoys the smaller and gentler hills, such as Bheinn Bheag a Deas (Little South Hill) to the back of our cottage, and the more or less level path walks that the islands offer in abundance. So, when she travels with me, I stick to those. When I'm alone, however, or with one or both of my sons, or with friends who come over from the mainland, the sky's the limit: literally, for I hope never again to finish a journey by helicopter.

About four years ago, I broached with the editors of *Am Pàipear*, the monthly newspaper of the lower Outer Hebrides, the notion of writing a column, in each issue, about my hill-walking experiences. To my surprise and pleasure, they accepted, and I have been writing the columns ever since. This book is a collection of those columns. The columns are running essentially as they appeared in the newspaper, except for minor corrections (as when I got distances or directions wrong in the original). Since there are only so many hills and glens to explore and write about, there is necessarily some duplication, and in a few instances the later pieces expand upon, or even modify, routes that I had suggested in earlier ones – the differences reflecting the fact that I had become more familiar with the territory in the meantime. (As an example: I now advise walkers who approach Stulabhal from the Mingearraidh valley to follow the north rather than the south side of the Thornaraigh River.)

My spellings of place names, I know, are hopelessly inconsistent. But then, so are the spellings you will find on maps and in guidebooks. Recently I have taken to using the Gaelic name first and then the English one in parentheses – this, in deference to a reader who argued that I was denigrating the local culture by favouring English names over Gaelic – but neither my Gaelic nor even my English spellings will always match the ones on the maps or in the guidebooks. Nor will they always match one another.

Please bear in mind that I wrote most of the columns from memory, back home in the States, with the assistance of only an ordnance map and a ruler. (The map I use is Explorer 453 from the Ordnance Survey series, 1:25 000 scale.) I have striven for accuracy, but cannot guarantee it. *Neither the publisher nor* Am Pàipear *nor I can accept liability for mistakes. Nor can we accept liability for mishaps.* Every hill-walker is responsible for his, or her, own safety.

I intersperse safety tips – helicopter-avoidance tips, if you will – throughout my columns, beginning with the first. The most important of all (it summarizes many of the rest) is: *stay focused; resist complacency.* On one of my earliest descents down Mhòr – descents being the most dangerous part of any hill walk, precisely because complacency tends

3

to set in – I found myself composing, and chanting to myself, a little ditty:

> *Don't get careless, don't get cocky;*
> *This old hill is steep and rocky.*
> *Don't get smart, don't get silly:*
> *Lots of ice on this here hilly.*

You won't always find ice on the Uist hills; indeed I've encountered much less of it in recent years than when I first started walking them. But you will find scree, which is just as slippery, bogs, hidden crevices and other surprises. The rhyme that I've recited to remind me of these potential surprises might be childish. But it has helped to keep me alert and safe.

The hills have given me a lot, as I hope the columns make clear. This book is partial payback.

1. A Visitor's Impressions

*Looking down at a rainbow from Thacla's (Hecla's) peak,
facing North*

THE first time I scampered up Ben Mhòr, in October 1987,
I wore sneakers and a light sports jacket, and carried
neither an ordnance map nor a compass. No mishap befell
me. I was lucky.

My luck ran out a decade later, when a Coastguard
helicopter winched me from the base of Mheall Mhòr at
3 am. The 'copter circled for an hour before descending.
One of the crew explained that its heat sensors could not
distinguish me from the sheep that were roaming the moor

at the same hour – until the crew figured out that a sheep's brains would give off more heat than mine, because a sheep had more sense. Point taken.

Since then, I have visited South Uist many times, built a holiday home there, and learned to respect its hills. I dress appropriately for hikes: lined wellingtons, cut to the knee, to keep me dry without slowing me down, and warm clothing, including gloves and a woolen cap, except in summer. (The cap, however, is *de rigeur* in any season.) I don't bother with an ordnance map, because I know the terrain well by now, but I do bring a compass in case I lose visibility in a sudden mist. I use a walking stick to help me ford streams and feel out what – if anything – is under the heather in front of me. I carry food (hard eggs, boiled potatoes, chocolate) and water, in a small rucksack – though I'm told that the water from the more distant lochs is perfectly potable, and have drunk it myself often without ill effects. I tell people where I'm going and for good measure leave a note next to the windshield of my car. Finally, I bring a flashlight or a cell phone: not that I expect to walk at night (too dangerous) or call for help in case of emergency (no service in most places), but at least I'll be able to make the helicopter's task easier if I should need its services again. I haven't needed them – but the remembered sound of its rotors motivates me when I feel my energies flagging toward the end of a long walk.

My favourite destination? I'm like the leprechaun in the musical *Finian's Rainbow*: the one I love best is the one I've last seen. If forced to choose, though, I'd probably opt for Hecla, 606 meters tall, with spectacular views, including one of Loch Corodale – a loch containing 'heavy water,' rarely found outside Scandinavia, of the sort used in nuclear reactors. Despite being slightly smaller than its southern neighbour Ben Mhòr, it is less accessible, as it is set back further from the roads. You can reach Mhòr's summit in an hour-and-a-half if you start from the Stoneybridge water station. But it takes an hour longer to conquer Hecla, even by the shortest route, which begins about a mile from the end of the Skipport road and extends for perhaps two miles, through rough country, until it brings you to a prominent ridge at the base of the hill, another half mile from the top (there is no path). The trek from the Drimsdale footpath, off the main road, is longer – four miles – but smoother, so that the walking time is almost the same. The path terminates twenty minutes into the walk, and afterwards you're on your own – with no help to be had from the compass, because a magnetic anomaly renders compasses useless on Hecla's slopes.

I, however, prefer a third approach, somewhat more arduous and time consuming than the others, but worth the added effort. Start from the improved Loch Skipport footpath, near the end of the Skipport road. Follow the path as it ascends, and then, shortly before it peters out, turn right across flat, often marshy, ground. You will come to a stream that meanders off to the right. It is no easy task to walk along either of that stream's rugged banks. But if you persist, you will be rewarded when the stream opens out suddenly into Loch Spotal, one of the island's hidden treasures, across from the dramatic palisades of Ben na h-Aire. Circle around the right – that is, the western – edge of Spotal and pick your way through the heather beyond it. You will see, to Hecla's left, a vivid green patch on the hillside. Climb the patch – it is steep but easily traversable – and you will end up just below and to the east of Hecla's craggy peak. My last time there, in a Force nine gale, I faced northwest – the direction from which I had come – and found myself looking *down* upon a rainbow, a thousand feet below me.

Beautiful as Hecla is, it has many competitors. I shall give details of those in future issues if my editors will indulge me.

Thacla (Hecla) is located almost midway between NGR NF 820 and 830 – slightly nearer to the latter – and NGR NF 340 and 350. All map references in this book are to Ordnance Survey (OS) Explorer 1:25000 no. 453 (Benbecula and South Uist), except for the references after article No. 28 ('Eaval'), which are to Explorer no. 454 (North Uist).

2. *Bagh Hartabhagh*

The ruins at Bagh Hartabhagh

'COME on, Dad, it's not as though we're climbing Everest.' So spoke my older son, with all the brash assurance of a teenager, when I urged him to step carefully as he, his younger brother, my wife and I set out last summer for Bagh Hartabhagh (Hartavagh Bay), two-and-a-half miles beyond North Glendale on the eastern edge of South Uist.

He had a point. After all, we weren't even hill walking. Rather, we were hiking across a low-lying, more or less level valley. There were hills on both sides of us – Cearsanais and Beinn Bheag (Little Hill) to the north, and Marabhal and Cruachan across Lochs Cearsanais and Marulaig to the south – but they interposed no obstacle. What they did do was to screen us in, so that we made our way eastward in utter solitude. There was also a path of sorts, although that is a courtesy title: wet and treacherous even in August, it functions, at all times of year, more as a guide than as a serviceable walkway. But at least it ensures that one does not get lost.

Extending past the ruins of the old South Glendale School on the left, the path stops abruptly at Broken Bridge, then resumes on the far side of Abhainn Marulaig. 'Abhainn' means either stream or river, and Marulaig is one or the other, depending on the season. Broken Bridge itself is aptly named, for the bridge that had once connected the two sides has long since toppled into the water. But there are stepping-stones a few yards south that will carry the hiker across – during the dry months, anyway.

East of the abhainn, the path winds and dips, until Bagh Hartabhagh looms ahead. Besides being a place of almost ethereal beauty, the bay is lined with the remains of cottages, some of them quite substantial, formerly belonging to crofters who had been 'cleared' there from the machair but could not sustain themselves in so desolate a spot. One does not have to believe in ghosts to feel the presence of their spirits.

The journey to Bagh Hartabhagh had taken us about an hour-and-a-half, which is par for the course, as I can attest from prior visits. I had wanted to press on further to the tiny promontory of Meall na h-Ordaig, which overlooks the Minch. ('Ordaig' means great toe, or thumb, and, gazing upon the oddly-shaped configuration, one can see how it got its name.) But my wife would have none of it, so we turned and retraced our steps.

It happened right after we had re-crossed the stepping-stones at Broken Bridge. Max, our older son, was trailing slightly behind us. Suddenly we heard a call for help. There he was, waist-deep in a bog, with one leg over the side, the other completely submerged, and his hand gripping the edge. Had he been alone, he would have been in trouble.

I now faced two dilemmas. The first was whether to memorialize his discomfiture by snapping a photograph or rush immediately to his side. My better nature prevailed. I rushed immediately to his side.

The second was whether to pull him out – or push him the rest of the way in. Again my better nature prevailed. With his brother's help, I pulled him out. Wiser for the experience, he no longer dismisses as inconsequential the hazards of walking on South Uist. Nor should he, for I have heard of others who have had near-death encounters with bogs, especially in that region.

The risks are well worth taking, however, because, except for a fish farm, the terrain is pristine, and the spectacle of the abandoned cottages can move, to the core, even phlegmatic types like myself who are not moved easily. Additionally, if you continue east for another 45 minutes to the crest of Meall na h-Ordaig, as I did on a later hike when I had no accompanying spouse to constrain me, you will be rewarded by a spectacular view of the sea. And the risks can be minimized by following the precautions I advised in my previous article: wearing boots, telling people where you are going, and using a walking stick to test out the ground in front of you.

A word to the wise: the stepping-stones at Broken Bridge are visible, and traversable, only during the dry months. From November through to March or April, when the abhainn is truly a river, the only sure way to reach Bagh Hartabhagh on foot is to start out from the bend of the road in South Glendale and proceed northeast across the moderate-sized hills of Cruachan and Thairtebreac. (Avoid the surrounding lowlands, which will be nigh impassable). Whenever you go, and by whatever route you arrive, you will behold, once you get there, what the late Boisdale poet Donald MacDonald described as 'wells that are deserted and the cold sites of houses…sights with your eyes to stimulate your thoughts.'

The ruins at Bagh Hartabhagh (Hartaval Bay) are located at NGR NF 830 and almost midway between NGR NF 150 and 160 – nearer to the former. The path from North Glendale begins somewhere between NGR NF 150 and 160 and NGR NF 790 and 800; I cannot plot it precisely. It is accessible from a spur that runs south off the North Glendale Road, near the terminus, but one must walk west over open country – uneven and wet – in order to find it.

3. *Mist Connection*

*The 'surpassingly beautiful' Loch Snigiscleit,
en route to Stulaval*

THE peak of Stulaval, 1,216 feet above sea level, is clearly
visible from our holiday home on North Locheynort.
Seeing it across the water, you would take it for the
easternmost of the South Locheynort hills, the others being –
in order, from the west – Sheaval, Trinival and Arnaval. (How
the ancient Norse names roll off the tongue!) Appearances,
though, are deceiving, for Stulaval actually stands well
behind those three, and is as near to its southern neighbour,
Triurebheinn, as it is to Arnaval.

There are many approaches to Stulaval by land, and I shall describe them all. But my first visit there, in August 2006, was by sea. And therein lies a cautionary tale.

Our friend and neighbor, John Joseph MacDonald, had brought my two sons – Max, 17, and Adam, 15 – and me in his boat and dropped us off near Kyle Stuley, on the island's eastern perimeter. The plan was that we would climb Stulaval and then continue northwest over Arnaval (835 feet) and Trinival (643) to the terminus of the South Locheynort road. Alternatively, we could proceed due west from Stulaval to the Thornaraigh River and follow its southern bank to the Mingarry footpath, which leads in turn to the main highway. Upon reaching one destination or the other, we would call home, where my wife – who does not share our taste for hill walking – was preparing dinner for awaited guests, and either she or one of the guests would collect us by car. The plan seemed eminently do-able, for it was only about four pm; we still had six to seven hours of daylight and the sky was clear except for one innocuous cloud in the east.

We scrambled up Stulaval's eastern slope, pausing every so often to turn and enjoy stunning views of Stuley Island and the Minch. As we neared the top, one of the boys said to me, 'Don't look, but that cloud has gotten bigger.'

It certainly had. Within moments, it had enveloped Stuley Island, and moments later it enveloped us, so that we could scarcely see one another, let alone our surroundings. Staying close together, we struggled through rain and mist to the summit, and reviewed our options.

There was no question now of returning over Arnaval and Trinival, for both were invisible. Knowing what I do today, I would have adopted the fallback plan of heading toward the Thornaraigh River, which winds through low ground around Arnaval's southern base toward Mingarry. But I had never explored that part of the island and, even with compass and ordnance map in hand, did not care to make its acquaintance in zero visibility. So instead we felt our way cautiously down Stulaval's west flank and, once at sea level, circled north around the western edge of Loch Snigiscleit. This loch, which we were seeing for the first time, is surpassingly beautiful, but we lacked leisure to savour its attractions. Our destination was the south shore of Loch Eynort, opposite Meall Mhòr, where I knew the ground. Although we got there safely, the detour added about two hours to our journey. When we finally reached the last house on South Locheynort, night had fallen, the food on our table was cold, my wife and guests were hungry and worried, and the helicopter crew at Stornoway was doubtless preparing another rescue mission.

Wishing never again to replicate August's experience, I made it a point during my next (November '06) visit to climb Stulaval from every possible direction and study the terrain. I found that if you go entirely by land, there are at least four approaches.

The shortest – about two-and-a-half miles and two-and-a-half hours each way – is from the end of the South Locheynort road past Arnaval's northern base. The walking is rough though.

If you're more ambitious, you can start at the same point and cross straight over Trinival and Arnaval, neither of which is especially challenging – as we were supposed to do, in reverse, on our journey back. The distance is about the same, the time also.

The other two routes are longer – about four miles apiece – but easier (and hence only fractionally more time consuming), because one involves very little climbing, and the other none at all, except for Stulaval itself. The former passes over the low ridge that separates Trinival from Sheaval; it then winds around Arnaval's southern base. The latter – again, reversing our August 'fallback' plan – is via the Mingarry footpath. When the path peters out near Loch nan Caorach, keep walking east to the Thornaraigh River and follow its southern bank until Stulaval looms ahead. One warning: in November, the short patch of ground between the path and the river is the wettest I've seen on South Uist. That's *wet*.

When you come to Loch Snigiscleit, pause to savour its attractions, for it is surpassingly beautiful. And the views from Stulaval's summit are superb. But keep a wary eye on the clouds.

Stulabhal (Stuleval) is located at NGR NF 810 240. The Mingearraidh (Mingarry) footpath runs to the right off the Mingarry Road, about midway between NGR NF 740 and 750 and NGR NF 260 and 270.

4. Hill-walking in June

South Uist's southeast coast, with Maol na h-Ordaig in the background

THOSE of you who have read my columns regularly, perhaps as penance imposed by a remorseless priest, might suppose that every walk I have taken on South Uist has ended in misadventure: a late-night helicopter rescue; a plunge into a bog; a blinding mist on a hilltop. The vast majority, however, have been uneventful – like the three I did on my latest visit this past June, when the island basked in an unprecedented spell of good weather.

The first walk was from the North Locheynort footpath to the further of the two hills that together comprise the oxymoronically-named Meall Mhòr (literally, Big Little Hill). The trick is not to follow the footpath to the end, but rather to turn left – that is, north – when it swings to the right after passing over a picturesque foot bridge. Otherwise you must circle around a long, steep-sloped peninsula, lengthening and complicating the journey. Still heading north, cross the isthmus on the east shore of Loch nam Faoileann and make for a fenced-in enclosure, the eastern boundary of which will lie in front of you and to your left. Do not enter the enclosure – keep it on the left – and after you reach it turn right as soon as you conveniently can. You will now be walking east, parallel to the loch. Another footbridge will bring you to an enclosed nature preserve, with a gate at each end and one more in the middle. Proceed obliquely through the preserve in a southeasterly direction. Upon exiting the last gate, you will find yourself at the base of the nearer and larger of the two hills. The easiest ascent is from the eastern side. The views from either hill are to die for. The distance to the further hill is about two miles, the walking time about two hours.

My second walk was the most ambitious of the three. Starting from the bend of the South Glendale road, I negotiated a series of enclosures and then a long stretch of open ground until I reached the very edge of the island's south-eastern coast, between Maol na h-Ordaig to the north and Rubha Mealabaig to the south. ('Maol' and 'rubha' both mean cape). This time I did not climb either eminence – been there, done that – but rather made for the low-lying ground in between. I also avoided the three mid-sized hills of Cruachan, Roineabhal and Thairtebreac along the way, skirting their bases rather than passing over their peaks.

I would not recommend this route at any time of year except the summer. Even in June, after more than two weeks of uninterrupted sunshine, the terrain at sea level was spongy in places, and in most other months it is quite impassable (been there, done that too). I have walked to Maol na h-Ordaig and Rubha Mealabhaig in wet seasons, but not easily, and only by keeping to the high ground.

Seen from atop the Maol or the Rubha, the coastal area that separates them appears almost flat. Not so when you're in that area looking up, as I was; there were all sorts of ridges and hollows, invisible from above, to impair visibility and slow me down. (I spent a frustrating 45 minutes, for instance, searching for a small loch, which, unbeknownst to me, was easily accessible just beyond the next rise). If Lord Raglan, Britain's commander-in-chief during the Crimean War, had absorbed that lesson, the Light Brigade would not have made its suicidal wrong-way charge at Balaclava.

The walk covered about three miles each way and took exactly six hours. I could have moved faster, but I was in no hurry, for there was ample daylight. The loch-studded locale is the most pristine and isolated on South Uist, and I wanted to savour it.

Finally, I made my annual pilgrimage to South Uist's tallest peak, Ben Mhòr, as I have been doing since 1987, when I was in my mid-forties. Eschewing the fastest route, from the Stoneybridge water station (one can also get there relatively quickly from the North Locheynort footpath), I set out instead from the improved footpath on Murdo MacKenzie's croft, which adds a mile and an hour in each direction, so that I was almost six hours getting to the top and back. Ben Mhòr is indeed a wondrous hill; every year it grows taller, its slopes grow steeper, and its base moves further from the roads on all sides. But the views from its crest are unchanging, and make the climber feel like a king.

◈

Meall Mhòr (Big Little Hill) is located about midway between NGR NF 810 270 and 280. The portion of the southeastern peninsula that this article describes is located principally at NGR NF 840, between NGR NF 140 and 150. Beinn Mhòr (Ben Mòr) is located near NGR NF 810 310; it covers a good deal more ground than that, of course, but this is where you will find the summit. The improved footpath begins to the right of the A865, immediately west of NGR NF 770 and about midway between NGR NF 340 and 350. The Stoneybridge water station is located at NGR NF 770, immediately north of NGR NF 320; one can drive right up to it from the A865. It looks down upon a standing stone.

5. *Lochs nan Arm and Spotal*

Loch nan Arm

THE principal downside to hill walking in August is the company. By that, I do not mean my 19-year-old son Max, whose companionship was delightful, and who managed this time to avoid sliding waist-deep into a bog, as reported in the June issue of this newspaper. I refer, rather, to the multi-legged company – midges and such – that elected to join us. In addition, after three weeks of uninterrupted sunshine a torrential rainstorm fell the very day we landed on the island (cause and effect, I guess), so the ground was soaked and we were grateful for our wellingtons. And where it was dry, we often had to fight our way through high heather, using walking sticks to test the invisible terrain below us. Nevertheless, we accomplished two spectacular walks.

The first required the aid of a boatman: our neighbour John Joseph MacDonald of North Locheynort, who deposited us at Kyle Stuley on the east coast of the island between Loch Eynort and Lochboisdale, whence we had once commenced our mist-shrouded journey over Stuleval, as reported in the July issue. But this time we by-passed that hill and instead made our way through Bealach ('mountain pass') Chaolais to the left, that is, to the south of it. This portion of the walk was relatively easy; a mostly gentle ascent through tall but yielding grass. Our destination was Lochboisdale.

Bealach Chaolais ends at Loch nan Arm, a small, shimmering gem, invisible almost until you reach it, that fairly exudes history and legend. Shortly before you arrive at its eastern shore, you will see (if you look closely enough), on the southeast side of the pass, an exposed souterrain: one of those mysterious man-made tunnels, of uncertain age, origin and purpose that burrow beneath so many of the glens. This one must have settled somewhat over the past 30 years, for whereas John Joseph had managed to crawl through much of it on his last visit there during the 1970s, I was only able to back in up to my thighs. (Of course, there is an alternative explanation for my inability to penetrate further – but I pride myself on being pretty slim). And a famous lochside battle is said to have taken place many centuries ago, between local MacDonalds and invading MacLeods from Skye, after which the survivors tossed their weapons into the water and erected a memorial cairn nearby. Alas, Max and I could not locate the cairn.

Some uncertainty now arose as to whether we should proceed along a nameless pass to the left of the loch, as I proposed, or walk around its southern shore and then veer southwest through yet another pass, Bealach na Diollaid, which runs between Stuleval and Triuirebheinn. Max, reading the map better than I did, advocated the latter option, and I followed his lead: a good thing too, as my route would have marooned us in the eastern glens. The bealach was rough going, for it rose steeply through tall, thick heather, but once we emerged from it Lochboisdale loomed to our left less than two miles away, and it was all downhill from there. The total distance was about three-and-a-half miles, the walking time about three-and-a-half hours plus half an hour seeking the souterrain.

The other long walk was to Loch Spotal, and it would have been even longer, to the very peak of Hecla, if my wife Beth had not accompanied us. Beth, however, has no taste for hill-climbing, or for marathon walks either, so we made Spotal our target. After a brisk initial ascent the route takes you across mostly level ground and the loch is exactly an hour from the Skipport Road. But there are challenges on the way. You first follow the improved Skipport footpath uphill almost to the end. Just before the path peters out, a few yards beyond a ruined cottage with a corrugated roof, turn right. You will now be going south, and the terrain is almost flat. Skirt the western shore of Loch Bein and then head south again until you reach a powerful stream. Turn right at the stream and inch forward for about twenty minutes along its western bank. You will struggle, for the slopes are steep and the surface uneven, and my cautiously probing walking stick did not prevent me from taking a scary tumble into a deep, water-logged crevice that lay concealed beneath the bracken. But soon the stream opens suddenly to reveal the stunning beauty of the loch, framed by the palisades of Beinn na-h'Aire on the far side, with Hecla rearing up immediately to the west. If your soul does not respond to that beauty, you have no poetry in you. But I bet you'll find that you have.

◈

Loch nan Arm is located about midway between NGR NF 810 220 and 230. Bealach na Diollaid extends between NGR NF 810 and NGR NF 220. Loch Spotal is located almost midway between NGR NF 830 370 and 380 – nearer to the former. One cannot miss the Sgioport (Skipport) path; it runs conspicuously to the right near the end of the Skipport Road, and is sign posted.

6. *The Flood Gate to Ben Tarbert*

The Flood Gate

IN my very first column for this newspaper, I wrote that I am like the leprechaun in the Broadway musical 'Finian's Rainbow': my most recent walk is always my favourite. Yet there are some that stand out in memory more than others. The walk across 'the Flood Gate' to the top of Ben Tarbert is one of them.

The path (for there is a path most of the way, although it is sometimes hard to see) begins just to the left of the last house on the Loch Carnan road, at East Gerinish. It forks almost immediately, and you really cannot go wrong whichever direction you follow. The left fork leads you zig-zagging, first downhill, then up, to a small eminence just below some ruined cottages. The sea is always visible to the east and the north, while Hecla looms to the south. If you don't fancy long, arduous walks, this may be the way to go, because it's a mere 45 minutes there and back, and the only obstacles are some puddles.

I, however, do fancy long, arduous walks – the more so the better – and thus I prefer to eschew the left fork and keep walking straight. This path soon swings to the right past a pair of sturdy old ruins, one of them a former factor's house to judge from the size, and appears to be taking you to the very base of Hecla. But it isn't, of course; Loch Skipport stands in the way. Instead, it continues curving, almost 180 degrees, so that whereas formerly you were heading more or less southeast, you are now going west. Another imposing ruin confronts you, even larger than the others; it is the foundation (complete with gates) of an ancient school, its walls extending to the Skipport shore. With a view like that, the pupils must have had a hard time concentrating on their studies.

Keeping the school to your left (after taking time to explore its interior), continue along the same westerly route. The path will appear to peter out moments later, about 100 yards north of several ruined cottages. But it doesn't. If you persevere, you will pick it up again on the far side of a bog. You would do well to walk around, not through, that bog.

When the path resumes, it brings you over open country, with Loch Skipport, now shrunken to a slim estuary, on your left. The landscape is dotted with more ruins, some of them in such excellent condition as to seem initially to be inhabited. At last you come to 'the Flood Gate': a tiny isthmus that separates Loch Skipport from Loch Bee. You can cross either the isthmus or a narrow, grooved metal footbridge immediately parallel to it. Choose the isthmus; the bridge can be slippery, and lacks railings.

Then the fun begins. Working your way through heather – there is no more path – proceed uphill till you reach the top of Ben Tarbert (Tairbeirt in Gaelic – it means 'isthmus'), about 540 feet above sea level. It is a stiff climb, but well worth doing. Facing south, you not only get a stunning look at Hecla, but its foothills reveal their secrets; you can clearly see Lochs Bein, Fada and Spotal, and other hidden jewels that are invisible from the roads.

The walk is about two hours each way. The one even moderately difficult part is ascending Tarbert. If you don't have four hours to spare, and want only to take in the view from Tarbert, its peak is 25 minutes from the nearest point on the Skipport Road. But if you're too rushed to spare four hours, why visit the Outer Hebrides?

*

I understand that some well-intentioned government and private groups hope to make the hills more accessible – hence more enticing – to tourists by installing directional cairns along the slopes. I respectfully disagree. The cairns, no matter how artfully designed, would mar the pristine beauty of the place. And I doubt they would attract more tourists, because the ones who need cairns to ease their way up mountains are not the sort to venture this far from the mainland, cairns or no. Even if they did come, moreover, they might drive out the present crop of visitors, many of them regulars, who are drawn here by the solitude and the challenge of finding their own way to the top – as well as by the pristine beauty of the place. For the improvement-minded, I suggest, instead, repairing the aptly-named 'Broken Bridge' to Bagh Hartavagh and restoring existing paths to their original condition, so that walkers can traverse them dry-shod. Let the hills remain as they are; we should not tinker with the work of their Architect.

◈

The Flood Gate is located almost midway between NGR NF 810 and 820 – nearer to the former – and slightly north of NGR NF 400. Beinn Tairbeirt (Ben Tarbert) is located slightly west of NGR NF 810 and almost midway between NGR NF 390 and 400 – nearer to the latter.

7. The Southeast: Rubha Mealabhaig and Sgeirr a Mhill

Rubha Mealabhaig

AS my friend Murdo MacKenzie of Snishival has admonished me, there are summer walks and there are winter walks, and I am not always smart enough to know the difference. About a year ago, I took a summer walk in the winter – well, not quite the winter, but early December, which is close enough – and almost carried it off: would have done, too, but for one mistake.

My destination was South Uist's southeast tip: Rubha Mealabhaig and, just beyond it, the two-pronged Sgeirr a

Mhill. Rubha means promontory – we settled that several issues ago – and nobody I know is quite certain what Mealabhaig means, except that its name is incomplete, like the craggy geological oddity that it describes. As nearly as I can discern, Sgeirr a Mhill means hills made of sea-rock, which is exactly what these are. They are even odder shaped than Mealabhaig. When I place Rubha Mealabhaig and Sgeirr a Mhill on the island's southeast tip, I am speaking literally, for one cannot go further, either south or east, without getting wet. One can also get plenty wet on the way there, as I shall explain. Neither formation is especially high, but each presents its challenges. Getting to them can be a challenge too.

I set out from the South Glendale road: more specifically, from the fourth house on the right counting south from where the road ends in a turn circle. The place is easy to spot, for there is a wide parking space by the road and a driveway that leads uphill to the house. Just past the house is the first of three barbed wire enclosures. Do not try to skirt them on the right: that is a good way to get very wet indeed. Instead, go straight through them. Each has stiles. From here, the target is approximately three miles southeast. Your route will take you along the coast; the Sound of Eriskay will be visible almost every step of the way. At this point, you cannot yet see either Mealabhaig or Sgeirr a Mhill, because Roineabhal, 201 metres high, blocks your view.

My common sense had not deserted me altogether, for I climbed over Cruachan, a smaller hill, rather than test the sponge-like low ground to its right. But when I came to Roineabhal, that common sense disappeared. I decided to walk around it, to the north – in other words, to its left. Big mistake. The sea-level terrain in the late fall is hopelessly boggy, and by the time I figured that out, the only way I could mount Roineabhal without backtracking was by its steep northern slope. Had I scaled it from the west, the ascent would have been relatively swift and easy, but this was neither. From the top, I could at last gaze through the distance at the spectacular hatchet-shaped western face of Mealabhaig, but I felt like Moses looking into Canaan: with limited daylight there was no chance of attaining the promised land – its peak – or of even setting eyes on Sgeirr a Mhill. I did, however, struggle to Mealabhaig's base, and climbed it part way, before giving up and returning to South Glendale. This time I did not try to cheat when I came to Roineabhal, and the passage across it from east to west was gentle.

On my next visit, in March, I had some unfinished business to attend to, so from the same starting point I proceeded southeast again. Chastened by my previous error, I did not try to skirt Roineabhal, but instead climbed directly over it without any difficulty. With daylight to spare, I attained both my destinations. It was worth the wait. To reach the top of Mealabhaig, one should follow the base south, almost to the Sound, then turn north, a full 180 degrees, and climb. The ascent is steep but short, and you will be rewarded with breathtaking views across a valley to Maol na h'Ordaig on the northeastern side of the peninsula and beyond it, across Lochs Boisdale and Aineort, to the majestic eastern hills: Kenneth, Triurebheinn, Stuleval, and Mhòr. Reversing direction once again, you can then march back down the slope to the Sgeirr. The further of the two knobs is shaped like a saddle, and if my wife had seen me scramble up it she would have been thinking eagerly about my life insurance.

I worried some as I worked my way to the edge, but if I'd slipped, at least I'd have died happy.

The total walking time is about three hours in each direction. My advice, if you go, is to avoid the mistake I made the first time: stay high and stay dry. Or do it in the summer.

Rubha Mealabhaig is located almost precisely at NGR NF 830 130; Sgeirr a Mhill is slightly to the southeast. Roineabhal (Roneval) is located at NGR NF 820 140.

8. *Winter Walks: Triuirebheinn and the Eastern Glens*

Triuirebheinn, from the dam at Loch nan Smalag

I HADN'T intended to climb Triuirebheinn (Triple Hill) on the shortest day of 2007. As I observed in the November issue of *Am Pàipear*, there are winter walks and summer walks. One should not climb even moderately high hills in winter, and Triuirebheinn, at 357 metres, surely qualifies as such. No: the ascent was an afterthought. Here is how it happened.

My initial, more modest agenda was to complete some unfinished business from the previous August, when my older son and I walked from Kyle Stuley, on South Uist's eastern perimeter, to Lochboisdale. After being dropped off by boat, we had proceeded west across Bealach a Chaolais (Pass of the Narrows) around the south side of Loch nan Arm ('Loch of the Weapons' – a legendary battle having once taken place there) and continued on the same westerly route along Bealach na Diollaid (Saddle Pass) below Triuirebheinn's northern face. We then descended, turned left and headed into town. I described the adventure in the October issue.

As the article mentioned, I had been intrigued by another, nameless pass, about halfway between the two we'd traversed, that extended southeast from Loch nan Arm's southern shore and led . . . I knew not where, except that it would deposit me in the eastern glens above Lochboisdale. This was, I believed, the only part of the island I had never visited before, so I determined, Columbus-like, to discover it. My plan was to switch direction by crossing Bealach na Diollaid from the west. That accomplished, I would follow the nameless pass, explore the eastern glens from north to south, and return via Coire na Cuilc, which separates Triuirebheinn from its southern neighbour Ben Kenneth. Coire na Cuilc is best known for the spectacular cave, high on its northern wall, where Prince Charlie, Neil MacEachen and Felix O'Neil may or may not have planned the Great Escape.

On 21 December I set out at dawn from the pedestrian causeway near Rubha Dubh, which I preferred to the one at Lasgair, just east of it, because I could drive almost to the water's edge. I knew I had barely six hours of daylight, and I'd estimated – correctly – that the walk would take very nearly that, so I wasted no time. I reached the western entrance to Bealach na Diollaid at 10.30 am. The descent to Loch nan Arm – its banks brown instead of the rich green I'd remembered – is challenging in any season, for the slope is steep and the heather thick. But by 11.30 am I was striding exultantly through the nameless pass, gateway to the hitherto unknown eastern glens, their mysteries awaiting me. Another 45 minutes of relatively gentle exertion brought me to the northern flank of Glen Nostapal. I would have to cross the glen to reach Coire na Cuilc.

I looked below, then at my watch, and did not like the odds. Nostapal's walls are high, in places almost sheer, and the only pass that penetrated the far palisade was a goodly distance to my left, which meant that I would have to reverse Columbus' itinerary by traveling east to go west. Glancing to my right, I saw, and on impulse chose, what looked like an easier alternative: a straight ascent that skirted Triuirebheinn just south of the peak. And so it proved, except for a seemingly bottomless bog at the top. Glancing right again, I noticed the peak immediately above me, thought 'why not?' and mounted it. And that is how, against my own counsel, I found myself moments later on the wind-swept summit, peering at Ben Kenneth, which was all but invisible through the mist.

The detour had, no pun intended, one downside: the descent from Triuirebheinn is precipitous, and I am no sheep. Once at ground level, however, I located the gamekeeper's path, which guided me swiftly back to the causeway. Worth it? You bet.

*

I essayed another walk this past December, and it was humbling: I accompanied John Hart, owner of Hebridean Jewellery, eastward along the southern face of Beinn Mhòr.

Winter or no, we'd aimed for the top, but there was too much cloud cover, so we probed Mhòr's eastern foothills – Beinn na Corach; Beinn na Tobha – instead. I'd thought myself agile, but John, an experienced climber, outdistanced me to the point where I felt like an awkward puppy stumbling after its master. That was humbling indeed. As I struggled to keep pace (with John pausing patiently from time to time to let me catch up), I realized I had never visited this area either. That too was humbling: whenever I delude myself into thinking I know the island intimately, it always surprises me with some new secret. May I be spared to uncover and report on others.

Triuirebheinn (Truireveinn) is located slightly east of NGR NF 810, about midway between NGR NF 210 and 220. Glen Nostapal extends from NGR NF 820 to 830, immediately below NGR NF 210. The map references for Bealach na Diollaid appear at the end of article No. 5 ('Lochs nan Arm and Spotal').

9. *Winter Walks*

Sheaval, from Trinival's peak

I HAVE written before about winter walks. As this is the last month in which the subject will be timely, I shall take the opportunity to describe two of my favourites.

Some prefatory cautions. First, the winter days are short (for instance, there are only six to seven hours of daylight in December – when the sun shines at all), so the walks should be short also. You don't want to be abroad at night. Second, the weather can turn nasty in an eye blink. That's true at any time of year – recall the fog that overtook my sons and me during a summer hike up Stuleval – but in winter it becomes *really* nasty. Do not, therefore, replicate George Bush's mistake in Iraq: have an exit strategy. Third, avoid the highest hills – Mhòr and its neighbours – for the temperatures up top can dip below freezing even when ground temperatures are mild and no snow is visible. And it's wise to keep civilisation in view, so you can signal with a flashlight if something goes wrong. (Definitely carry a flashlight – or a cell-phone, which can serve the same purpose – but do not count upon the latter for making emergency calls, because many places off the beaten track lack service). The following two walks meet all these criteria.

One of them takes you up the adjacent hills of Sheaval (223 metres) and Trinival (198 metres) on the south side of Loch Eynort. Mind, neither hill is easy. Both have steep ascents, pesky barbed wire fences, and false peaks (Trinival's even has a cairn on it) that make their summits seem closer to the road than is actually the case. Still, they are not as tall as the other hills I have mentioned, or as Arnabhal (257 metres) on their left, and unless you push your luck by venturing down their south slopes you are never far from the comforting sight of the South Locheynort houses.

To conquer Sheaval, the more westerly of the two, drive east along the South Locheynort road till you come to a left-hand bend. Park there, off the road, and walk for about five minutes in the same direction towards a small old house on your right. Uphill from the house is a gate where two fences intersect. Make for the gate and walk through it. Sheaval's peak, or what appears to be Sheaval's peak (it isn't really; the true peak is behind it), will now be on your left. Do not, however, head directly towards either peak, for the ground is boggy. Instead, proceed obliquely right, to the hill's western base, and climb the ridge to the trig point at the summit. The walk takes 45 minutes.

It is another 45 minutes from the trig point to the true top of Trinival by the shortest route, across Bealach Sheaval (Sheaval Pass) along a line of old fence posts. To get to the Bealach, though, you must scramble down Sheaval's steep and sometimes slippery eastern slope. The south-eastern descent is easier, but lengthens the journey somewhat and propels you further from those South Locheynort houses. From Trinival back to your car is, again, 45 minutes.

The views, both from the tops and along the way, are perhaps the island's most stunning because, the hills being relatively low, the landmarks are clearly visible. To the south, loch-studded Glen Labasdall stretches toward Lochboisdale; Eriskay, Barra and Mingulay lie beyond. To the north, across Loch Eynort, looms Beinn Mhòr, at 620 metres the highest hill on the archipelago. To the east, past Stuleval (374 metres), Loch Eynort empties into the Minch. But the grandest spectacle of all is west and northwest, over the machair to the Atlantic, where on a sunny day one can see the Monachs and St. Kilda.

Another favourite winter destination is Easabhal. Tallest of the hills below Lochboisdale, at 243 metres, it is nevertheless easily accessible if you do it right. Drive toward South Glendale past the Eriskay causeway and next past a lone white house, both on your right. Turn left immediately afterward onto a short gravel road – there is one macadam patch – that ends at Easabhal's base. Park, and then follow the natural contours of the terrain. They will lead you on a zig-zagging course to the top. 'Top' is perhaps a misnomer, for Easabhal is unique in having no peak; rather, the summit consists of a long, wide plateau, extending from Ludag to South Lochboisdale, the true top of which is difficult to discern. (Previous sojourners have left multiple cairns). Here too one enjoys excellent views, especially east over Roineabhal and Thairebreac to the Minch. The plateau is broad enough to provide a sense of isolation, but one is always within reach of surrounding villages. Enjoy. Stay safe.

Seabhal (Sheaval) is located immediately west of NGR NF 770, where it straddles NGR NF 270. Trinneabhal (Trinival) is located immediately southwest of NGR NF 780 270. The principal part of Easabhal's (Easaval's) mass is located between NGR NF 770 and 780 and NGR NF 150 and 160.

10. *Sheaval and Hecla*

Younger son Adam, seated atop Sheaval's trig point

IT was mid-March. And the weather on South Uist was foul. But I repeat myself.

Nevertheless, the skies lightened long enough for my younger son Adam and me to do two hill walks. The first was to Sheaval, on South Locheynort, 223 metres high; the second, and more ambitious, was to Hecla, at 606 metres the archipelago's second tallest eminence.

We did not set out for Sheaval until mid-afternoon on Monday, 10 March, when the morning's rain and hail finally ended. Initially we proceeded as I had advised in last month's issue: uphill from a tiny, vacant old house that is located just beyond the left-hand bend on the South Locheynort road, then through a gate where two fences intersect. From there, the path of least resistance would have been to turn right and hike along level ground to the base of a gentle rise on Sheaval's western flank. The next and ultimate lap would have had us reverse direction and follow the rise to the two peaks, the larger of which, invisible from the road, stands directly behind the other. This might seem counter-intuitive: why not continue from the gate to the top in a straight line? The short answer is that the longer route avoids some nasty bogs and a steep ascent over thick, unyielding heather.

Adam, however – 17 years old, and an accomplished athlete – eschewed the path of least resistance. He wanted a challenge, so nothing would do but that we brave the heather, the steep ascent and the bogs in a frontal assault. Despite these obstacles, the journey to the top and back took just 40 minutes each way, which was slightly less than I'd estimated in last month's article. What's more, I beat Adam to the summit. Here's how. As we approached the trig point, he was well ahead of me. I asked him to wait, and, when I caught up, I told him that if he looked west he would see an amazing geological phenomenon. While he was looking for it (there is none) I snuck ahead and touched my walking stick to the monument.

We climbed Hecla the next morning. We agreed that there would be no unnecessary challenges, and no competition either, for the climb is challenging enough, and one's competitor is the mountain. Moreover, time was at a premium, for although the day dawned brightly, our neighbour John

Joseph MacDonald had warned us that the weather would turn at around 1 pm.

In different circumstances I would have left from the Drimsdale telephone station off the main road, or used the Loch Skipport footpath and then skirted Loch Spotal, these being the most beautiful ways up. But they are slow, and, with the forecast in mind, I wanted to reach our destination quickly. Accordingly we started instead from the second passing place after the forest on the Loch Skipport road. (The next two passing places would have served equally well). Due south lie three ridges that extend semi-circularly, one after the other – bending first southwest, then southeast – towards the peak. If one crosses directly over them, Hecla's distinctive crown is but a short distance off. Normally the walk takes two to two-and-a-half hours, but the ground was wet – *bha e glè fhliuch gu dearbh!* – plus, we made a mistake: thinking we saw a short cut, we mounted the second of the ridges, Maol Daimh (Friendship Mound), from its eastern side instead of marching straight across it. We were wrong; there are no short cuts on the hills. As a result, I did not attain the summit until exactly 1.00 pm – two hours and 55 minutes after we'd begun. Adam got there a few minutes sooner. Our detour aside, we'd been buoyed much of the way by the reassuring sight of other human footsteps.

John Jo's prediction was right on the mark: the rains also hit the summit at exactly 1.00 pm. We had hoped to scramble down to Loch Corodale, in Glen Usinish, and collect a sample of its fabled 'heavy water' – the kind used to propel nuclear reactors – to bring for analysis to Adam's high school chemistry class. Speak of challenges, how would we have explained the water's function at customs when we returned to the States? But the question never arose, because the rain put paid to the plan, and we returned to the Skipport road as rapidly as prudence allowed. This time we essayed no short cuts, so we arrived in two-and-a-quarter hours. There was one untoward episode, when I slipped in a river and the water flooded my wellingtons. If the temperature had dropped below freezing the consequences could have been dire, but it didn't, so they were merely unpleasant, and I was spared – hopefully, to write more hill-walking articles.

The map references for these locations appear at the end of articles No. 1 ('A Visitor's Impressions') and 9 ('Winter Walks').

11. *The Three-Hill Walk*

The three hills: from Hecla's peak, looking south across Corodale to Bheinn Mhòr

IT'S spring, with summer waiting in the wings, which means that the season is right for the Big One. I refer to the three-hill walk across South Uist's tallest eminences – Hecla (606 metres), Corodale (527 metres), and Mòr (620 metres) – which extend north to south, one after the other, between the Loch Skipport and Loch Eynort roads.

I've done it twice: first in mid-March of 2002 (which probably wasn't a good idea, but I survived), and then in early June of 2005. The approximately six-mile trek took me seven-and-a-half hours the first time and nine hours the second. This might seem odd, because the ground is wetter in March, making progress more difficult. I like to think that the reason for the difference was not that my faculties had declined in the interim but rather that in 2002 I was alone whereas in 2005 a friend accompanied me. The friend, a mere 60-year-old, was several years younger than I was, hence not yet in his prime, and he slowed me down.

Bear in mind, however, that what constitutes the three-hill walk is a matter of definition. For instance, several locals have told me that they managed it in about five-and-a-half hours. Initially I was jealous, but then, using my lawyer's training to cross-examine them, I discovered that they had finished at (or started from, if they did it in reverse) the Stoneybridge water station off the main road. Uh-uh: that's not fair. The true test is from side road to side road: Skipport to Eynort, as I went on both occasions, or else the other way around. That adds at least an hour to the journey.

I approached Hecla from the same direction on each of the walks – the direction I described in last month's issue – and I advise others to do likewise. Starting from the second, third or fourth passing place after the Skipport Road forest (any of them will serve), proceed south toward Maoil Daimh, which is the second of three ridges that rise in succession toward Hecla's summit. (Maoil means hill; daimh has several meanings, but here appears to mean deer). As I wrote in April, there are more scenic routes, but they take longer, and even in summer one should not be too prodigal with one's time. Several streams block the way, but they are passable, though you may have to search patiently for the fords. Climb directly over those three ridges; do not try to avoid them! It is two to two-and-a-half hours from the road to the peak.

Getting from there to Corodale is tricky, and will take another one-and-a-half to two hours. The most direct way, almost due south, is a no-go, for the hill's northern flank is nigh unassailable unless you have climbing equipment and know how to use it. (I haven't and don't). Instead, you need first to scramble down into the western extremity of Glen Usinish, keeping Loch Corodale, with its fabled 'heavy water,' well on your left. Corodale's distinctive knob will now loom in front of you to the southeast. Ascend gradually – you will pass gem-like tiny lochs halfway up – but do not head straight toward the knob; you cannot mount it from that side either. Rather, walk below it until you reach the hill's southern shoulder, then circle back (that is, north) and climb along that shoulder to the top. Your grandest view will be east into Glen Corodale, enclosed by the imposing palisades known as Cas fo Tuath and Cas fo Deas (North Leg and South Leg respectively), where Charlie hid after Culloden. His exact abode, only the ruins of which remain, is invisible from the knob, concealed beneath a slope that drops sharply to the Minch. That is why he chose it. Although you will not see his living quarters, you may in season see eagles.

Going from Corodale to Mòr is not easy either. The descent is so precipitous that on the 2005 excursion my friend and I negotiated a portion of it on our backs. From the base, you should cross a land bridge across Sheileasdall Pass to an equally steep rise. Once at the top of the rise, it is still a stiff southeasterly walk to the summit. The Locheynort road is now clearly visible, but your difficulties are not over, for you must pick your way carefully through the scree on your way down. When you near sea level, follow the fence line south, continue along the eastern shore of Loch nam Faoileann to the public footpath, and you're home.

But have a ride waiting for you to bring you back to your car on the Skipport Road. Exhilarating though the walk will have been, you will not want to replicate it in reverse.

Since this walk extends from road to road, map references are probably unnecessary, but I shall provide some anyway: the walk begins, from the Skipport Road, at approximately NGR NF 810, and ends at the terminus of the North Loch Aineort (Locheynort) Road, slightly above NGR NF 280 and slightly west of NGR NF 790.

12.   *Hill-walking on South Uist – Corodale*

Corodale's 'distinctive crown'

BEN Corodale's 'distinctive knob,' as I called it in the last issue – like a crown rather than your typical conical peak – is not the mountain's only remarkable feature. Smallest (527 metres) of the three adjacent eminences that bisect South Uist north to south between Lochs Skipport and Aineort, it is nevertheless the least accessible: the most precipitous, and the furthest (approximately three-and-a-half miles) from the nearest road. It is also the most steeped in history, for behind the knob lies the spectacular sheltered glen, of the same name, where Charles Edward Stuart alternately skulked and reveled from mid-May through early June of 1746, after his flight from Culloden.

The easiest way up (that adjective is relative) is via the improved public footpath that runs from the main road – the A865 – past an abandoned mill house. When the path ends, continue east over open ground in the direction of the knob. As I cautioned in May, remember to ascend towards the knob from its right (that is, from the south), rather than frontally or from the left; otherwise you will only wind up descending and then mounting from the right after all, and you might as well do it sensibly the first time. It will save you at least half an hour of wasted effort. Although I have climbed Corodale in every season (including, imprudently, one winter when there was deep snow at the top), it has been several years since my last visit and I no longer recall precisely how long the walk took me: at a rough guess, two-and-a-half to three hours. The views from the knob are dramatic indeed: to the north, Hecla (606 metres); to the south, Ben Mhòr (620 metres) and beyond it the southern isles: to the west, the machair and then the Atlantic; and to the east, Glen Corodale and the Minch, with Skye in the distance. But the best is yet to come.

If you do the walk in spring or summer (not in winter, when there is insufficient daylight!) you can proceed down into Glen Corodale and re-trace Charlie's footsteps. The glen is a geological marvel, bisected by a burn that empties into the Minch, and enclosed by a pair of nearly sheer, tentacle-like palisades: Cas fo Tuath (North Leg) and Cas fo Deas (South Leg). Charlie is said to have hidden in a cave that penetrates the northern face where the glen drops toward the Minch, but knowledgeable locals are sceptical. His true habitation was a forester's cottage, only the foundations of which are still visible, on rising ground, in the glen's southeastern corner. Do not confuse these with the much better preserved remains of clearance houses that were built in the nineteenth century and then abandoned when their occupants gave up and moved on to Eriskay. Those houses can be observed from the knob; Charles's bolt hole was more cunningly concealed beneath the slopes of Creag Fhudair, which hugs Cas fo Deas near the latter's eastern extremity.

For adventurers who are both persistent and lucky, there is now a special treat in store: if you can locate the correct cornerstone of the forester's house, and are strong enough to lift it, you will see underneath one of the souterrains, or man-made underground tunnels, that have snaked below the eastern glens from time immemorial, with nobody knowing who constructed them, or when, or why: escape hatches? Jails for captured enemies? Places to store food away from the penetrating eyes of marauders? This particular souterrain runs only a short distance, expanding at one point into what looks from above like a subterranean chamber, before exiting into a small cave at the base of Cas fo Deas; the exit is concealed by another boulder. One can crawl through the tunnel, but I do not advise it, for the last time I looked it was already occupied, by that staple of West Highland landscapes: decomposing sheep carcasses. Whether it was built specially for Charlie, or preceded his visit by centuries, I cannot say.

It is about a mile-and-a-half, and an hour (for the descent is gentle), from the knob to the Minch, so the entire walk – from the A865 to the Minch and back – takes perhaps eight hours. If you have another half hour or so of daylight, treat yourself to an additional thrill: meander onto Rubha Hellisdale, a peninsula that extends hook-like into the

Minch at the glen's terminus. In season you may see seals cavorting in the water and, in the opposite direction, eagles soaring over the knob. And if the light is propitious, you may even, who knows, see the watchful ships of the old Royal Navy, landing parties at the ready to scour the glen at the first sighting of the Stuart Prince.

Beinn Corrodail (Ben Corodale) is located almost precisely at NGR NF 820 and NGR NF 330. Gleann Corodail (Glen Corodale) – curiously, the map gives it only one 'r' whereas the hill has two – extends from NGR NF 820 to 840 and from NGR NF 320 to 330. Rubha Sheileasdail (Hellisdale Peninsula) ends slightly beyond NGR NF 840, almost midway between NGR NF 300 and 310 – nearer to the latter.

13. *Island Path Walks – Rueval to Rossinish*

The sea coast at Rossinish

MY monthly column is usually entitled 'Hillwalking on South Uist,' but except for one digression this article is about neither. Rather, it describes the level three-mile path walk from the A865 to the Rossinish peninsula on Benbecula.

The walk begins, unpromisingly, at the island dump site, which one passes (as rapidly as possible) on the left. The digression rears up immediately afterward: Rueval, which at 124 metres (about 400 feet) is Benbecula's tallest hill. It is worth a detour. Don't turn off the path to climb it until you are well south of it; otherwise you will encounter boggy ground even at the driest times of year. It is at most half an hour from the path to the top.

Although Rueval is tiny compared to the majestic eminences of neighbouring South Uist, the terrain around it is completely flat, so your views are unimpeded on all sides. If you're a history buff, you will want to gaze west at Nunton House, where the Clanranald chiefs removed themselves after Ormiclate Castle, their ancestral home, burned down in 1715. There, slightly more than thirty years later, Lady Clanranald and the legendary Flora MacDonald schemed to spirit the fugitive Charles Edward Stuart over the sea to Skye. From this same vantage point atop Rueval, Charlie also gazed west at Nunton House, impatiently waiting for the ladies to send word that the bonnie boat was ready. The more dramatic views, however, lie south, across Loch Hermidale toward Hecla (the Askernish artist Bill Neill has made a fine lithograph of that one), and southeast, toward Loch Uiskevagh, from the far shore of which the bonnie boat finally sped out to sea.

To save yourself time, do not retrace your steps going down; instead, descend via Rueval's eastern slope. The angle is mostly gentle, and you can rejoin the path soon after reaching the bottom.

You will then face a difficult choice, for the path forks at Loch Deighe fo Dheas. (I have been unable to translate this: 'fo' means 'under' and 'Dheas' means 'south,' but none of the definitions I have found for 'Deighe' makes sense in context.) The choice is what self-help gurus call 'win-win': you can't go wrong with either. The southern path, which peels off to the right, is shorter (about a mile and a half from the junction). But it is also wetter and not as well delineated; indeed, during the summer it disappears altogether under thick reeds, so that you will think you've reached its terminus when in fact it resumes once you've fought your way through them. It then winds past a pair of sparkling fresh water lochs before culminating at a disused pier just beyond the ruined foundation of a large building that was once used as a holding area for incoming sheep. Next to the pier is a standing stone.

If you want to see Rossinish, though, keep going straight, along the northern branch. There are some wet areas here too, and you will have to circle off the path to get around them, but you will be rewarded by impressive distant views of Eaval and the Lees on North Uist. The path narrows, hugging the edge of a low cliff above the water (don't worry; it isn't as scary as it sounds), then ends at an estuary that has no name on the ordinance map.

The journey up to this point will have taken you about an hour-and-a-half, if you've bypassed Rueval, or two-and-a-quarter to two-and-a-half hours if you've climbed it. You can now either call it a day and turn back, or press on to Rossinish.

If you press on, the best is yet to come. Cross over a short isthmus – the ground here rises slightly, but is easily traversable – and you will be on the peninsula. My first sight of it surprised me, for I had heard it described as the most desolate and isolated spot on the entire archipelago (which is why Charles skulked there whilst awaiting the finalization of his escape plans) and I had imagined it as a gloomy moonscape, covered with forbidding brown heather and saturated with bogs. But no: it is flat, open and grassy, with a magnificent white sand beach on its eastern shore, well-preserved ruins of what must once have been substantial houses, and breathtaking views of North Uist. Rossinish is about a mile across at its widest point, or slightly more than three miles in circumference, and despite the absence of a path you cannot get lost if you circle the coast, for eventually you will return to the isthmus. If memory serves, you can complete that circle in about two hours. Worth the additional time and effort? No doubt about it. I'm surprised Charlie could tear himself away.

This walk begins about midway – indeed it seems, from the map, almost precisely midway – between NGR NF 800 and 810 and NGR NF 530 and 540, and ends, if you press on through Roisinis (Rossinish), immediately beyond NGR NF 880 530.

14. *Summer Destinations*

Max and Adam leaning against the standing stone at Loch Uiskevagh's Scaraloid Bay

BY the time this issue hits the shops I shall have been on the islands for two weeks, and I shall remain for one week more: my longest-ever stay. My family – wife Beth, and sons Max, 20, and Adam, 18 – will join me at different times. Where shall we walk together?

With Beth, the options are limited. Living with me is challenge enough; she needs no others. Our hikes, therefore, will be short and mostly level: the north footpath at the East Gerinish end of the Loch Carnan road, leading to some ruined cottages and the sea (45 minutes round trip), the improved Skipport footpath that extends from the end of the Skipport Road towards Loch Spotal (an hour each way if you go the additional distance from the path to the loch), and the southern fork of the Rueval footpath to the pier and standing stone at Scaraloid Bay on Loch Uiskevagh (an hour-and-a-half each way – the limits of her tolerance) are the furthest she will venture. Perhaps I can coax her up Rueval on Benbecula (124 metres), Sheaval on South Loch Eynort (223 metres), or flat-topped Easabhal near the southwestern edge of South Uist (243 metres) – I have described them all, in detail, in previous articles – but they will be more difficult sells. The boys and I, however, crave redder meat.

To them, and to first-time tourists, I propose the following destinations, in no particular order. Again, I have previously written separately about each.

HECLA (606 metres). Shortest route (two-and-a-half hours in each direction): proceed south from the second, third or fourth passing place beyond the Skipport Road forest to Maoil Daimh and continue southeast to the peak. Longer but more scenic: circle the western shore of Loch Spotal (to get there, see above) and mount a distinctive bright green patch of hill to Hecla's eastern shoulder. Or, from the west (this is the furthest – four miles each way – but also the gentlest): start at the Drimsdale phone station by the A865, follow a footpath till it ends, and keep going east till you reach the top.

MHÒR (620 metres – tallest in the archipelago): I'm going to try a different way up this time, via the new trail that extends westward from the public footpath on north Loch

Aineort. At its terminus, cross a three-tiered stile next to Loch an Dorain and head straight for the hill. After about half a mile, turn east and walk along a level ledge that runs below, and parallel to, the summit. When you arrive at Mhòr's eastern flank, reverse course and resume climbing. The zig-zagging seems counterintuitive, for it lengthens the distance, but it avoids some steep ascents. Likely one-way time: two-and-a-half-hours.

STULEVAL (374 meters): the easiest and most scenic route is also the longest (four miles, three hours each way), but it's level up to the base. From the end of the Mingarry footpath (detour to inspect the burial cairn on your right) make for the Thornaraigh River and follow it east past Arnabhal (257 metres), which will be on your left, till you see Loch Snigiscleit, also on your left. Stuleval will loom just ahead.

LOCH NAN ARM: from one of the Lasgair causeways, walk northeast in the shadows of Ben Kenneth and Truirebheinn to Diollaid Pass, an hour away, then take the pass, keeping Truirebheinn on your right, to the tiny loch. After skirting its western and southern shores, exit through another, nameless pass that runs more or less southeast, and go due south through the remote eastern glens. You can return to Lasgair either over Truirebheinn (357 metres) or, if you don't fancy climbing, via the pass to its left, beneath its southern slope; or you can carry on, first to the next glen and then, turning right (west), through Coire na Cuilc with its storied cave. Allow six hours total.

THE SOUTHEASTERN PENINSULA: From the fourth-to-last house on the South Glendale Road – its driveway runs diagonally uphill to the right – go east through a pair of fenced-in areas (there are stiles) over Cruachan and Roneval (no shortcuts; the low ground is wet) to hatchet-shaped Rubha Mealabaig on the island's southeastern tip. Next, stroll north across level terrain to Rubha na h'Ordaig, South Uist's easternmost point, and savour the views of the northern hills. To complete the triangle, either follow the path that runs west through the haunted ruins of Bagh Thairteabagh and over the stepping stones at Broken Bridge till you reach a spur that brings you back to South Glendale, or climb over Thairteabreac and Cruachan (again, no shortcuts!) till you see the enclosures. You'll need seven hours for this one.

THE SOUTHWESTERN LOCH CARNAN FOOTPATH, through 'the Floodgates' to Ben Tarbert (168 metres), overlooking Loch Spotal across the Skipport Road: two to two-and-a-half hours each way.

I have other ideas, but these will keep us busy. And you.

I have provided most of the relevant map references after previous articles. Scaraloid Bay, which one reaches by taking the right – that is, the southern – fork off the Rueval footpath, is located immediately southeast of NGR NF 850 520.

15. *July and August*

Max atop Ben Corodale in the mist

I HAVE been in our Loch Eynort holiday cottage for nearly three weeks now, and my family has joined me in shifts: first, wife Beth and younger son Adam, who turned 18 here, and then Max, our older, who is 20. In my August article I had listed half a dozen lengthy walks I'd hoped to take with the boys (Beth having no interest in such). We have, in fact, taken several of them, plus some new ones.

Two of the walks involved Ben Corodale (527 metres), the centrepiece of the three hills that bisect South Uist north to south, the others being, in order, Hecla (606 metres) and

Mòr (620 metres). Though Corodale is the smallest, it is also the most difficult, because it is the steepest and furthest from the roads. I shall describe both Corodale walks below; the others must await the October issue.

My first, with Adam, was a new one for me. It began when friends dropped us off by boat at the shingle beach in back of Hecla, just below the bothy, on the east coast of the island. From there we passed through Glen Usinish, where we walked around Loch Corodale, famed for its heavy water (used in nuclear reactors), and picked up a sample to bring home to America for analysis. We then crossed over Ben Corodale's peak and made for the main road, the A865, via the improved footpath at Mill Croft. Logically we should have circled the north shore of Loch Corodale, then climbed Corodale via a relatively gentle ridge at Glen Usinish's western extremity. But Adam wanted a challenge, so nothing would do but that we scramble up the almost sheer side of Cas fo Tuath – the daunting palisade that stands between Glens Usinish and Corodale. (Confusingly, Loch Corodale is in the former.) Feeling like the Persians seeking a path at Thermopylae, we clawed our way to the top. From there we walked across level ground to Ben Corodale's distinctive knob, where we paused to admire the soaring vistas, the most magnificent of which extended northeast past the shingle beach to Nicholson's Leap. After descending Corodale's steep western slope, we struggled through undulating heather and bog toward the A865.

I made two mistakes. First, I wore boots instead of hiking shoes, which was foolish, for the ground was mostly dry, and the boots weighed me down. Second, I forgot that to reach the improved footpath one must keep Ben Corodale fully visible at one's back. Instead, we let ourselves drift to our left, till all but its peak had disappeared beneath the slope of Ben Mòr. In consequence, we emerged south of the path, and had to slog our way through a final mile of nasty (undulating, boggy) terrain.

The walk covered five-and-a-half miles and took the same number of hours. In candour Adam could have shaved at least half an hour from the total if he'd been alone.

The second Corodale walk, with Max, followed a route I'd taken many times before, from the Mill Croft footpath to the Minch and back: five miles, four hours each way – three-and-a-half miles, three hours to Corodale's peak, plus a mile-and-a-half and an hour from there to the shore, and the same in reverse. When I last did it twelve years ago, I needed only seven hours, but the hill seems to have grown since then. Profiting from my previous error, I wore hiking shoes instead of boots, but this time the ground was wet, so the shoes, saturated with water, weighed me down as badly as the boots had done, and my feet got soaked besides. At least, though, I had sense enough to keep Corodale directly behind me when we returned. This brought us back to the path, which made that final mile much easier.

Like Adam, Max outpaced me, and could doubtless have completed the walk in seven hours on his own. I vividly recall fighting my way out of Glen Corodale – where every ridge conceals another, steeper one beyond it – and hearing him shout to me from the top, which he attained far ahead of me, 'Thalatta! Thalatta!' ('The sea! The sea!'). No Greek mercenary of Xenophon's felt more joy at the sound.

How do summer walks compare to spring, fall and winter ones? There are trade-offs. Summer affords more daylight, but at a price: heat and midges. The ground is drier (that's relative!), but it can nevertheless be spongy, and the grass and heather are taller. These conditions made nearly every step arduous – for me if not for the boys.

Stay tuned for the other walks that they and I took together. Unless, that is, U.S. customs scrutinizes the bottled water too closely, in which case my writing privileges may be curtailed for some years to come.

Again, I have provided most of the relevant map references after previous articles. Loch Corodail (the map gives it only one 'r', same as the glen) is located at, and around, the intersection of NGR NF 830 and NGR NF 330.

16. *Hecla in August*

To Hecla from Drimsdale: Maol Daimh straight ahead,
Hecla behind it at its right

IN previous issues I have suggested several ways to climb
Hecla (606 metres), northernmost of the three tall hills
that separate the machair from the eastern glens. I have
now chosen my favourite (at least until I next try one of
the others). It's the route I described in my very first article
for this newspaper: the one that begins at the Drimsdale
telephone station just off the A865. I did it alone in March
2007, and again this past August, accompanied by my older
son Max, 20, and a visiting friend of mine, from the Isle

of Man, whose age must remain a state secret. I was able last time to observe the terrain and landmarks much more closely than in '07 – probably because on the earlier occasion I fought my way, imprudently, through driving sleet in what locals later told me was a Force nine gale, with winds of above fifty miles an hour on the ground and heaven knows how much more powerful aloft. (I recall being afraid to stand up on the top.) In August, however, we enjoyed clear, calm weather, and I made notes along the way.

From Drimsdale to Hecla is four miles. That is considerably longer than any of the Skipport Road approaches, which range from two-and-a-half miles to about three. But the Drimsdale route is the easiest, hence quickest, of the lot. There are no impediments: no unpleasant surprises in the form of un-fordable streams or hidden dips followed by steep re-ascents. Instead, you have a series of gentle rises connected by level plateaus that you can cross rapidly and almost effortlessly. The principal challenges, in August anyway, were high heather and spongy ground: ground which, as Dave, my friend from Mann, put it, suggested a thin crust floating on interminable bog, and produced a similar sensation to walking on sand. We reached the peak in just two-and-a-half hours – in '07 I had needed three, but the wind and weather must have slowed me down – and Max could have done it in two if we oldsters had not encumbered him. The Skipport routes, shorter but more difficult, take at least that, and some take longer.

From the telephone station, proceed for about fifteen minutes along a footpath that swings right over a footbridge and ends at a gate that opens onto a grassy hillock. From there, the important landmarks will be clearly visible most of the way. Behind you, as you ascend, are the three western settlements of Howmore, Drimsdale and Stilligarry, with Howmore to the south and Drimsdale the centerpiece of the three. All you need do, to avoid going astray, is to keep Drimsdale at your back and Hecla's crown in front, so that you are walking an almost straight line between them. About a mile-and-a-half in, the terrain will fall away to reveal an unsuspected glen, then rise and fall away once more to reveal another. Each contains a pair of breathtakingly beautiful lochs, separated by an isthmus. (We drank from those lochs, without ill effect; I would be less trustful of the ones nearer the road.) Cross each isthmus, and, after the second, make for the base of Hecla's foothill, Maol Daimh. Pass over it – despite a rough beginning, its surface is mostly smooth and level – and you're there. I cannot promise you a rainbow a thousand feet below, as I experienced in '07, but I do promise some of the finest views on the island.

*

I described, in the July issue, a hike to Rossinish, in eastern Benbecula – one of Prince Charlie's hiding places – along the level Rueval footpath from the A865. Thanks to the Hache family (visitors who, like myself, own a holiday home), I discovered another approach that cuts an hour from the time and adds some excitement along the way. Starting from the end of the Flodda island causeway, cross Kyle Flodda – at low tide only, of course – to an old shieling, proceed south until you join the footpath two-and-a-half miles east of the main road, and follow it from there. (If the tides catch you short, circle the Kyle's western shore instead.) After the first or second gate (I forget which), take a short detour south, toward Meanish, where you will encounter a ruin with walls so thick as to suggest much greater antiquity than a shieling or crofthouse. Jean Didier Hache, the family patriarch (and author of 'The French MacDonald,' an excellent book), believes it dates to Neolithic times and is keen to bring in archaeologists to find out. Knowing him, I'd bet he's right.

The Dreamasdale (Drimsdale) footpath begins at the A865, slightly west of NGR NF 770 and slightly north of NGR NF 370. I have provided the location for Hecla at the end of article No. 1 ('A Visitor's Impressions').

17. A Cautionary Tale

Showing Beth the crime scene: Meall Mhòr, approximately where the helicopter found me

IN Scottish history, 1792 was *Bliadhna nan Caorach*, the Year of the Sheep – the beginning of the Highland Clearances. And 1745 was *Bliadhna a' Phrionnsa*, the Year of the Prince, when Charles Stuart launched the last Jacobite rising. Their associations are not pleasant.

For me, 1997 was *Bliadhna nan Helicoiptear*. The term needs no translation. Its associations are likewise not pleasant, to me or to the hapless locals whose sleep I caused to be disrupted. Mine is, in fact, a cautionary tale.

I'd wanted to visit Glen Corodale, where Charlie skulked after Culloden. Instead of climbing over Ben Corodale from the A865 – see my June and August articles – I chose a different approach: from the end of the North Locheynort Road through the eastern glens. I did almost everything wrong.

I carried no ordnance map, compass or torch. Nor did I bring a walking stick, which is not essential but can make long hikes easier, especially on rough terrain. For warmth, I wore just a flimsy summer jacket. Though I had a sweater in the car, I left it there, thinking the April temperatures too balmy for it. That was true during the day, but even in April the nights can be freezing. Of course, I didn't expect to be abroad at night. However, I was wrong about that, and was lucky that on this particular night the temperatures held at four to five degrees Celsius.

I did not leave a note on my dashboard, stating where I was going and when I would return, or tell anyone. About the only thing I did right was to carry light snacks and water. That was lucky also.

The adventure commenced auspiciously. From the Locheynort Road to Glen Corodale is nearly four miles. I followed the Locheynort footpath almost to the end. Then, striking out over open country, I crossed Bealach Crosgard (Crosgard Pass) between Ben Mhòr's eastern flank and Ben nan Caorach. Upon descending into Glen Liaddale, I headed east to the coast, where the ground was relatively level. Once there, it was less than a mile, due north except for the undulations of the coastline, to my destination. I reached the glen four hours after exiting my car, which local hill-walkers tell me is around par. Eyeing my watch, I spent another hour happily exploring the glen and the adjacent Rubha (Cape) Hellisdale. I had six daylight hours to return to the car.

As George Bush might have said: mission accomplished. Right.

My travails began on my homeward journey. As I approached the spot where I should have left the coast and retraced my steps to Bealach Crosgard, my legs started to tire, and I didn't fancy pushing them over Ben Mhòr's formidable foothills. So instead I circled the coast on what I thought would be an easy detour. It was not. If I'd consulted a map, I'd have realized that I was going nearly three miles out of my way – enough to eat up the daylight – but I had no map. A compass might have alerted me to my folly – but I had no compass.

The light faded as I approached Meall Mhòr's northern slope. That is where I now know I was, but I didn't know then, or indeed for some years afterward. At this point I was barely an hour from my car, and could probably have gotten to it even in the gathering darkness, but I didn't know that either. Despairing of progressing further, I scrambled down to sea level, hunkered inside a burn, and prepared to spend the night. I stayed awake, lest the temperatures freeze, and, shivering in my summer jacket, diverted myself by contemplating Hale-Bopp's comet, ablaze in the southern sky.

The Coastguard helicopter began circling noisily overhead at about 2 am, awakening sleepers miles away. Archie MacDonald, owner of the last house on Locheynort, had summoned it towards midnight upon seeing my empty parked car. I should have helped the crew to locate me, and to conserve fuel, by signaling my whereabouts with a torch. But I had no torch. It was another hour before the heat sensors detected me. Once they did, the 'copter swooped down, hovered, winched me aboard (that was my scariest moment) and deposited me at my car, whence I drove to my hotel, the Borrodale. To my mortification, the worried staff had left their beds to receive me.

Recently I was chatting with a New Hampshire mountain guide here in the States. We were comparing the dangers of the New Hampshire and Scottish hills. There are differences – New Hampshire's have no heather, bogs, or hidden crevices – but there is one common denominator: the climbers most at risk are those who are oblivious to risk. As I was. Not anymore.

The map references for Glen Corodale appear at the end of article No. 12 ('Corodale'). The map references for Meall Mhòr appear at the end of article No. 4 ('Hill-walking in June'). Bealach Crosgard (Crosgard Pass), known locally as Shepherd's Pass, is located slightly southwest of NGR NF 820 300.

18. *Beinn Mhòr in December*

Beinn Mhòr in winter – note ice patches just below the peak – from the new footpath

I STATED in my December 2008 column that I would do no major hill walks during my forthcoming visit later in the month.

But I did.

For the past year I'd yearned obsessively to complete an aborted walk that John Hart, of Hebridean Jewellery, and I had attempted in December '07. John had shown me a novel route up Beinn Mhòr: one that took advantage of the trails that Archie MacDonald has recently driven westward from the North Loch Aineort public footpath. Hitherto, when approaching Mhòr from Loch Aineort I had followed that footpath across the stiled bridge, then veered off and proceeded straight toward the mountain, skirting the east coast of Loch nam Faoileann and walking alongside a deer fence (keeping the fence on the left) to the base. The ascent from there, though linear, was dauntingly steep.

John and I, however, forsook the public path just before the bridge. Instead, we headed west along one of the new trails till we came to a multi-tiered stile – terrifying to acrophobes – at Loch an Dorain. Crossing the stile into gently rising open country, we made for a level ridge that hugged the mountainside below and parallel to the crest. The idea was to join the ridge directly underneath the peak, and, turning right (that is, southeast), walk along it until Mhòr's eastern shoulder dipped enough for us to resume our climb. Once on the shoulder, we would reverse direction again until we reached the trig point at the summit. Our zig-zagging course would increase the distance, but would also avoid the steep ascent from the Loch Aineort side.

Alas, the summit that day was mist-shrouded. So, abandoning our objective, we stuck to the ridge and contented ourselves with exploring Mhòr's foothills. I reported the adventure in my February '08 article.

This time I resolved to do better. And on Christmas Day I succeeded.

Throughout the previous week I had tried and failed almost as often as Robert the Bruce. There was mist on top, or I had started too late, or a suspicious storm cloud loomed behind me. I therefore turned back. In retrospect I could probably have made it each time, but took no chances; as my readers know, I'm helicopter-averse.

Although Christmas morning was overcast, I judged, correctly, that it wouldn't rain. So I set out at daybreak, wearing boots and carrying a walking stick, for the ground was soaked from recent downpours. It is fifteen minutes from the beginning of the public footpath to the Loch an Dorain stile. Once past it, I walked straight ahead over a low rise to a barbed wire fence. No problem: the barbed wire had been removed from the three sections immediately in front of me, so I crossed comfortably. Beyond, slightly to my left behind a heather patch, was a narrow footbridge, conspicuously marked on its far side by a red circlet atop a post. I crossed that too.

At this point I erred. I was now facing Mhòr dead centre, but, wishing to avoid precipitous climbs, I swung obliquely left towards Tigh Iarras Pass. I needn't have bothered: the direct approach would have been just as gentle, as I later verified going down. The deviation cost me approximately twenty minutes. Either way, the ridge was easy to reach and recognize: as an American judge famously wrote about obscenity, I can't describe it, but you'll know it when you see it, for it hugs the mountain wall. Roughly two-thirds of a mile southeast the crest slopes downward, at which juncture I abandoned the ridge and worked my way up. That final rise was challenging, with several false crests. Nevertheless, the journey as a whole was less taxing – albeit no faster – than the alternative route via Loch nam Faoileann.

Ultimately, I didn't attain the true top (the trig point) but halted upon reaching the easternmost cairn. As that is on the crest, I deemed it close enough given the season and the high winds that assailed me aloft. Total time (without the deviation): about two-and-a-quarter hours each way.

My wife fantasizes that when I die our two sons will carry my ashes to Mhòr's summit and scatter them. (I do not know whether her fantasy includes expediting the event.) I suspect that the brutes will do no such thing; rather, they will dump the ashes into a bog at the base and scamper joyfully to the top unburdened.

That would be a fitter memorial.

Loch an Dorain is located almost midway between NGR NF 790 and 800 – nearer to the former – immediately north of NGR NF 290. Loch nam Faoileann is located immediately west of NGR NF 800; it straddles NGR NF 290. Other relevant map references appear after previous articles.

19. *Wiay*

With Beth and the boys atop Beinn a Tuath on Wiay

I WROTE last December that – having either visited, or seen from adjacent eminences, every corner of South Uist and Benbecula – I felt like Alexander the Great in believing that I had no worlds left to conquer.

Those words were a gauntlet at the feet of my friend and fellow *Am Pàipear* columnist Alasdair MacEachen of Aird. So, during my Christmas week visit, he showed me a world that I had not yet discovered: Wiay.

Wiay (pronounced 'Wee-ah' – the 'y' is silent; in older sources, 'Ouia'; in Gaelic, *Fuidhaigh*) is a tiny island, perhaps a mile-and-a-half square, which lies about half a mile east of Peter's Port, Benbecula. To reach it, of course, one needs a boat and boatman, and Alasdair provided both in the person of his neighbour Ken Wilson. Ken, a retired Agricultural Officer, holds the shooting rights on Wiay, and while we were there made good use of them: after seeing us safely ashore, he went off on his own and returned at the day's end with a plump woodcock in hand.

The drive to Peter's Port along the B891 is worth taking for its own sake. For the last mile or so, there is no habitation whatever: the terrain, as desolate as any I have seen in the Outer Hebrides (at least, any that is accessible by car), is hauntingly beautiful and gives one the sense of being on an alien planet. After a rapid succession of some half a dozen causeways, the road terminates abruptly at the port, which is located on Benbecula's southeastern periphery. The 'port' – really, just a pier – is described in Ray Burnett's 1986 book, 'Benbecula,' as 'derelict and in disrepair.' But that pier, a wooden one, is gone, and in its place is a concrete slipway that local fishermen use daily.

My wife Beth, our sons Max (20) and Adam (18), and I met Alasdair and Ken on the pier at daybreak on Boxing Day. I was by then fully recovered from my successful assault on Beinn Mhòr the previous day (as reported in the January issue). With Alasdair and Ken was surgeon Des O'Callaghan, who lives at Nunton when he is not busy saving lives in a northern English hospital. I was surprised that Beth had accompanied us so willingly, because she has no taste for hill walking or arduous hiking. She believed, however, that the day's itinerary would not be taxing. Little did she know.

Landing on Wiay was no easy exercise, for there was neither harbour nor dock. But with Ken's help we scrambled safely ashore to the south of Rubha nan Ron ('Promontory of the Seals'). This was a spectacular introduction to the place, for the terrain rose steeply from the water, its surface a carpet of heather burnished in reddish brown winter colours. Upon reaching the top, we set out to explore, with Alasdair in the lead. The island is in many ways a microcosm of the archipelago. It has two respectable hills: Beinn a Tuath ('North Hill'), 102 metres, and Beinn a Deas ('South Hill'), which is slightly smaller. Surrounding them are numerous lochs, each a sparkling gem.

The island's best-known feature, though, is a low cave, called Leabaidh a'Phrionnsa ('the Prince's Bed'), reportedly occupied by the fugitive prince Charles Edward Stuart in early June 1746. Don't believe it. Charles and his companions – one of them Alasdair's collateral forebear Neil MacEachen – definitely spent two or three days on Wiay immediately after search parties forced them out of Glen Corrodale. (A militia troop, assigned to hunt him, landed on Wiay during that period; it may even have spotted him and chosen to ignore him.) But he is unlikely to have used the cave, any more than he used the even more famous one in Glen Corrodale itself. Certainly none of the companions recorded his having done so.

Alasdair's connections to Wiay, incidentally, run deep, for his great grandfather Malcolm MacRae and his family were its last occupants, having taken on the lease from Lady Gordon Cathcart's estate in 1912. The island's present owner plans to restore the onetime MacRae home for use as a holiday cottage.

The visit's high point, literally and metaphorically, was attaining Beinn a Tuath's summit and savouring the views. The climb was strenuous despite the hill's modest size. Beth, to my surprise, bore the ascent uncomplainingly and even seemed to enjoy it, though she was out of breath at its conclusion. I'm hoping next to coax her up Mhòr. Meanwhile, I'm getting ready for my forthcoming March visit – to begin about when this issue hits the shops – and contemplating what old worlds to rediscover and new ones to conquer.

NOTE: *I thank Alasdair, not only for the excursion, but also for assistance with this article.*

The pier at Port Pheadair (Peter's Port) is located almost midway between NGR NF 850 450 and 460 – nearer to the latter. Fuidhaigh (Wiay) is centered at NGR NF 870 460.

20. The Gamekeeper's track to Corodale

The ATV track snakes east past Beinn na Tobha;
note the winching track in the background

AS readers know, I've a dismal record walking from Loch Eynort to Glen Corodale. The first and, hitherto, the only time I'd tried it, in April 1997, I returned to Loch Eynort by helicopter after getting lost below Meall Mhòr.

Last month I finally redeemed myself. I negotiated the eight-mile round trip entirely on foot.

What emboldened me to seek redemption? I know the terrain somewhat better than I did the last time. Despite being twelve years older, I'm probably fitter now. I've learned to carry a walking stick – an energy saver and potential life saver. Most importantly, I benefited from a new ATV track, constructed by gamekeeper Alasdair Scott, which connects the two points.

The track originates at Loch Olaidh an Ear, just off the main road. The most painless way of joining it from Loch Eynort is to proceed towards Mhòr via the route I described in February. From the Loch Eynort public path, follow the new trails west to the three-tiered stile at Loch an Dorain. Cross the stile. Then, pointing straight at the mountain, pass over a low ridge and through a barbed wire fence. (Where the fence forms a right angle, several sections of wire have been removed.) In front of you, slightly to your left, is a footbridge, clearly marked by a red circlet atop a post; cross that also, and carry on towards the mountain. Climb one more ridge, then glance ahead and to your right: you will see what looks like another footbridge. But it isn't; it is a railed ramp, one of several that the gamekeeper uses to winch his ATV over especially difficult terrain. You have found the track.

A warning about these ramps. They can serve as footbridges, but shouldn't: the surfaces are slippery, and you could break a leg by falling between the rails. Find ways around them.

I reached the ramp just before 9 am, forty minutes into my walk. Turning right, I followed the track east, facing the rising sun – which blinded me, but I had no alternative: to complete my itinerary before dark, I had to set out early. The track is not the most direct way to Corodale – it might not even be the fastest – but it is, literally, the path of least resistance, for it winds sinuously in order to avoid the higher elevations. After exiting the valley, it continues east beneath the rugged north face of Beinn na Tobha: a landscape as stark as Tolkien's Mordor. Then, about an hour and forty-five minutes into the journey, it nears the Minch, at which point it swings sharply north for what looks like a gentle two-mile victory lap along the coast and into the glen.

But the lap isn't gentle, nor does it always follow the coast, for the track's undulations often carry it inland, lengthening the distance. In places, moreover, it disappears, or seems to, although I was able to rejoin it further on. At last it ended beside some ruined houses at the eastern extremity of Cas fo Deas: the palisade that separates Glen Corodale from its southern neighbour Glen Hellisdale. The Cas is not steep here, and I was able to enter Corodale at exactly 12.35 pm.

I now faced a decision: how to go back? I still had six hours of daylight, but that hadn't been enough in 1997. I wasn't sure I could find the track again, or follow it if I did, and landmarks I'd memorized carefully had either vanished or become unrecognizable from afar. The helicopter's rotors buzzed in my imagination. I flirted with returning over Ben Corodale to the A865 – no walk in the park, but a route I knew intimately – and even took steps in that direction. Then, a mile off, I saw one of the ramps, and bounded towards it happily.

Curiously, I was able this time to follow the path without interruption, perhaps because the afternoon sun illuminated even its fainter contours more than the morning one had done (though there were a couple of scary moments when I thought I'd lost it, and – since I'd reversed direction – that sun too blinded me). I was in my car at 5.45 pm, having squandered a half-hour by foolishly leaving the track to pursue a seeming short cut around Loch nam Faoileann.

I am agnostic on the charged question of whether these tracks should be permitted. People I respect inveigh against them as excrescences upon the landscape, and having myself denounced other so-called improvements (proposed directional cairns, for example), I understand their feelings. Let me say, in muted defence, that this track – a mere shallow impression, really – seems minimally intrusive. And it may have spared me a close encounter of the second kind with the dreaded helicopter.

Loch Olaidh an Ear is located between NGR NF 760 310 and 770 310; in fact, it straddles the east-west coordinates. Loch an Dorain's map references appear at the end of article No. 18 ('Beinn Mhòr in December'). The track's terminus at Cas fo Deas is located at approximately NGR NF 830 310.

21. Hill-Walking on the Southern Isles – Rueval

Rueval, from the south

IT was Saturday, March 14, the final day of my latest visit to the islands, and I had about two hours on my hands before I had to be at the airport. I dutifully deposited my household rubbish at the 24/7 skip off the A865, and looked around. Beyond, due east, was the Rueval footpath, with Rueval itself on the left. I had walked both many times. On this particular afternoon, I hesitated to do either, because the weather was foul: wind, mist, and incessant cold drizzle. But it beat boozing away the two hours at a local bar, so I set out, still uncertain whether I would tackle the hill or merely follow the footpath until time ran short.

Initially there was no question of climbing, for there are deep peat bogs, between the path and Rueval's base, which one would not want to cross in any season. But before long I had left the bogs behind, the summit loomed to the north, and the intervening terrain seemed obstacle free. So I thought, why not? – and, veering left, I made for the top.

Despite the drizzle – indeed despite the rains that had drenched the islands for nearly a week – the ground was remarkably dry: fortunately so, since I had left my walking stick and hiking boots at the Loch Aineort cottage before closing it up for the season. There were wet spots, true, but I could easily avoid them as long as I kept my eyes open. From the path to the top was just twenty minutes. Upon reaching it, I experienced my one unpleasant surprise: the wind picked up so viciously that it nearly bowled me over. But I regained my balance and, once used to it, was able to walk comfortably.

Though Rueval is tiny compared to its huge southern neighbours – the ordnance survey lists it at 124 metres – the rest of Benbecula is completely flat except for a few even lower-lying hills atop distant eastern islets (which anyway are not part of Benbecula proper). In clear weather, therefore, the views are spectacular: east and west, to both coasts; north, to the Harris mountains; and south over Loch Hermidale to Hecla (a scene that Askernish artist Bill Neill has memorialized). On this very summit Charlie lurked, as I was doing, during his final hours in the Outer Hebrides, before he boarded the Bonnie Boat at Loch Uiskevagh; from here he peered anxiously west at Nunton House, waiting for

Flora to emerge and cross the machair. He would have had no difficulty seeing Nunton House, or Loch Uiskevagh either, but alas, both were hidden from me – Harris and Hecla too – by the ever-present mist.

I did not tarry, for the clock was ticking. Instead of re-tracing my steps, I struck out almost due east, and descended via the hill's eastern shoulder. This is more precipitous than the southern slope that I'd taken going up, but it is not treacherous if one is careful. The descent too consumed twenty minutes. Rejoining the path about half a mile from where I'd left it, I was soon back at the skip, where I'd parked my car. Total walking time (including time on the path): seventy minutes. Despite the weather it was a nice coda to my eight-day visit.

Rueval is small enough so that climbers are unlikely to get lost except in an especially thick mist. (The mist that I encountered only impeded distant views; at no point did it threaten to obscure the sight line between the summit and the path, or I wouldn't have climbed.) But if they are ever in doubt as to the best way up, there is now one of those ubiquitous ATV tracks – mixed blessings, as I explained in my last article – to guide them. Unlike other hill walks that I have described, this one requires only moderate fitness.

*

On the morning of that same day, I received an object lesson in how easy it is to become lost. Thinking of climbing the big fellow – Mhòr, on South Uist – I approached it from the Stoneybridge water station, but after half an hour I saw that clouds had enveloped the summit, so I turned back. To my dismay, I could not locate the water station, for, from that perspective, each foothill seemed very like the rest. I finally exited about a hundred yards south of it, and might have gone even further astray if I had not had the new Cothrom building to use as a reference point. I was never in danger – one way or another I would eventually have reached the A865 – but it could have been a different story had I been in the eastern glens (where compasses can be unreliable). Be wary.

◈

Ruabhal (Rueval) is located almost exactly midway between NGR NF 820 and 830 and NGR NF 530 and 540.

22. Hillwalking on South Uist – Summer

From Stuleval's peak, looking north across the mouth of Loch Aineort

AS I write this column, I'm gearing up for my forthcoming summer stay in our Loch Aineort cottage – to last, I anticipate, for about a month. I haven't booked flights yet, but am excitedly checking the calendar. I'll purchase tickets soon.

Summer is ideal for walking on the islands, because the days are long and the ground is relatively dry. I don't always care for the company, by which I mean midges, rather than fellow hikers, but the midges leave you alone if it is windy, or once you get high enough. (When I speak of getting high enough, I refer to altitude, not to controlled substances – although I suppose that the latter might also be helpful in that one would notice the midges less.) Mind, there are hazards even in summer: a sudden storm, or a mist like the one that stole up and blinded my kids and me atop Stuleval two Augusts ago. One can minimize those risks, however, by checking weather reports and carefully scanning the sky.

So, how shall I take advantage of the long days and relatively dry ground? I have three objectives. Once I've achieved them, all else will be day-to-day.

The first is contingent upon whether my eighteen-year-old son Adam joins me for part of the visit and has the necessary stamina for the venture. (Just kidding: Adam, a strapping goalkeeper who guested for Iochdar last summer, has stamina to spare.) Or if not Adam, a friend from the Isle of Man, closer to my own age, who frequently comes over to go walking with me. We would replicate the expedition that I described in this newspaper's April issue: from the north Loch Aineort public footpath to Glen Corodale, eight miles and nine hours there and back, via the gamekeeper's ATV track that originates below Beinn Mhòr. You follow one of the new footpaths west from the public path, climb over the three-tiered stile beside Loch an Dorain, and, pointing straight at the mountain, walk north until you reach the track. You will cross a footbridge on the way. The track will bring you the rest of the distance: first below stark foothills, often encased in shadow (the track's builder cleverly avoided the higher elevations), and then along the eastern coast. Remember to walk around, not over, the railed ramps that you will encounter; their purpose is to carry the ATV above streams and bogs, not to accommodate pedestrian traffic. They are treacherously slick when they are the slightest bit moist, and you would not want to risk breaking an ankle or leg by slipping between the rails. But if Adam, or Dave (my friend from Mann), does not join me, I'll probably forego the Corodale jaunt: been there, done that.

Alone or accompanied, I definitely intend once again to climb Stuleval, which at 374 metres towers in back of south Loch Aineort. There are many ways of approaching it, but the easiest (albeit the longest: roughly four miles, three hours, each way) is from the Mingarry footpath off the A865. When the path ends, strike out east across open country till you come to the Thornaraigh River. (A cautionary note: that open country can be boggy even in high summer, and is nigh impassable at other times of year.) Then, still going east, follow the south bank of the river to the hill. You will be rewarded with stunning views of Loch Snigiscleit, which I count among the most beautiful lochs on the island. If time allows, you can descend Stuleval's far side and explore the haunting ruins at Caolas Stuley on the east coast, or, turning south, visit tiny Loch nan Arm, which rivals Loch Snigiscleit in beauty if not in size.

Lastly, I mean to treat myself to the three-point walk from South Glendale to the hatchet-shaped palisade of Rubha Mealabhaig on the island's southeastern extremity, then north to Maol na h'Ordaig on the peninsula's northeastern edge, and finally back to South Glendale (total distance, about seven miles; time, six to seven hours). You start from the fourth-to-last house on the South Glendale road – it is easily recognised, for a steep driveway rises obliquely to its right. Proceed through a fenced-in field (there are plenty of gates) across the adjacent hills of Cruachan and Ronabhal, and return over Thairtebreac, perhaps stopping to view Bagh Thairteabhagh – another cluster of haunting ruins – along the way. Don't try to skirt the fenced-in field or the hills: bogs await you.

I have taken these walks before, and never encountered a soul. Perhaps this time I shall. If that is a result of reading this article, I shall feel amply rewarded for having written it.

The relevant map references have all been provided after previous articles, except for Maol na h'Ordaig, which is located at NGR NF 840 160.

23. 'Modest' path walks

Beth and Max at Loch Spotal, which is accessible from the Skipport path

I WAS born and raised in New York City, but never visited the Empire State building. After all, it would always be there, right? Neither did I visit the World Trade Center. It too would always be there...

So I'm not surprised when friends on South Uist or Benbecula acknowledge that they have never ventured onto the hills, or through the trackless eastern glens, of either island, for these would always be there. Nor was I surprised when one such friend recently sent me an urgent request. Two friends of his were arriving from the mainland and wanted to attempt some modest walks. He could not suggest any, for he had never taken any himself; why should he, when the opportunities would always be there? Did I have any ideas?

Well, yes. And, since the walks were to be modest, the ideas centred upon the truly spectacular, but little-utilized, public footpaths on both islands. I'll describe a few of them, as I did to him, in no particular order. All have ample parking nearby.

The Loch Skipport improved path runs south and then east from near the end of the Loch Skipport road. It rises steeply after turning east, but even a moderately fit person can handle the ascent. My wife, who dislikes long walking, has done this walk often and enjoys it immensely. It's about 25 minutes from starting point to terminus: the limit of her endurance. (One can slog from the path to Hecla, 606 metres above sea level, but that is literally and figuratively a taller order.)

Another of my wife's favourites is the Locheynort public footpath, which begins at the end of the North Locheynort road. It first winds through a small forest. Upon exiting the forest, it opens onto spectacular views of the loch and the northern Locheynort hills – Ben Mòr to Meall Mòr – before crossing a cleverly-designed footbridge and finally petering out a little to the east. This walk, too, is about 25 minutes each way. These days you can enhance it by exploring a network of new footpaths that radiate outward from it, both east and west, before you reach the bridge. You will not get lost on any of them, for they all eventually rejoin the original one. (I have discussed them in previous issues.)

My wife also favours the Mingarry footpath to Loch nan Caorach. From the A865, take the Mingarry road almost to the end. The footpath runs obliquely to the right past a dam, on the left, and a Neolithic cairn, on the right. Also on the right is a tiny hill, perhaps a hundred feet high, with its own path to the summit. Though the hill is small, the surrounding terrain is flat, so there are excellent views, especially north and east. Again, allow 25 minutes, each way, for the footpath, and another ten each way if you climb the hill.

The Rueval footpath on Benbecula begins unpromisingly at the skip off the A865. But the scenery and air quickly improve. The path meanders east for a mile-and-a-half, and then forks. You can follow it to the fork, or take a quick detour up the southern slope of Rueval (a mere 124 metres), descend via the eastern slope, and rejoin the path there. (See my May '09 column.) At the fork, you have more choices. You can turn back. You can take the left prong, which brings you east for another mile-and-a-half till the path ends at Rossinish. (That walk, however, is not 'modest' – especially if you carry on into Rossinish itself.) Or you can take the right prong – shorter, but wetter and less well marked – which leads southeast to Scaraleode and Loch Uiskevagh.

The footpath that begins at East Gerinish (where the Loch Carnan road ends) also forks. The left, or northern, prong is another favourite of my wife's; it passes through a field, then zig-zags northeast to some ruined houses near the sea. Its total walking time is about the same as for the Skipport, Locheynort and Mingarry paths. That, plus its wild beauty, is why it is a favourite of my wife's. The right prong, which leads southeast to the 'Flood Gate' (the tiny isthmus that separates Lochs Skipport and Bee), is a more ambitious undertaking –one hour each way – but the committed hiker will find it worth the effort.

More ambitious still is the path walk from North or South Glendale to the ruins at Bagh Hartavagh. For that reason, and also because I have described it in past issues (and am running out of space), I shall not describe it here.

If you're new to the islands, try one or two of these paths on this, your first visit, then come back and do the rest. They'll always be there.

Either the relevant map references have been provided after previous articles or their locations are evident from ordinary road maps – usually both.

24. *Stulaval Revisited*

Stulaval, from the valley east of Mingearraidh

MY summer visit to these islands is more than half over. Soon I must return to Connecticut, where I shall pore wistfully through my many photographs. They will remind me of my latest conquests, much in the way that dry war banners, suspended from cathedral ceilings, evoke past battlefield glories. Stulaval. Easaval. Ben Mòr (three times – four if you count one occasion when cloud cover forced me back just shy of the top). Layaval. Shuravat. Askerveinn. Eaval, on North Uist. Truireveinn and Ben Kenneth (the latter two in the same afternoon). Thanks to nigh-unremitting sunshine, I collected material for several articles. I shall focus, in this one, on Stulaval.

In light of my recent experiences, I must revise some previous observations.

First, I had proclaimed summer the best season for walking. Mmm. 'S maithead. True, the days are longer, so you shouldn't get stuck on the hills at night – and, even if you do, you're unlikely to get hypothermia. Also, the ground is relatively dry (though, as I've remarked before, the key word is relatively). But there are trade-offs. The grass and heather are taller: in places, almost impenetrably so. And then there are the clegs. (That's a new word for me; where I come from they're called horseflies.) As tormentors, they put midges to shame, and they can be dangerous as well as annoying, because they deflect your attention from the ground. Fortunately, they are slow and easy to kill; trouble is, you cannot possibly kill them all. The only other good thing about them is that they don't come out when it's windy. Since most days on Uist are windy, even in the summer, you've a decent chance of escaping them.

Second, I had said that the easiest way to Stulaval – albeit the longest – is to take the Mingarry footpath and then follow the south bank of the Thornaraigh River to Stulaval's base: a level trek of some four miles. (It's just three miles each way via the South Locheynort hills, but you're constantly climbing and descending.) No. The sole advantage of following the south bank is that you avoid crossing the Thornaraigh. The ground, however, is awful: full of the tall grass and taller heather that I mentioned in the preceding paragraph, and boggy besides, with only the occasional sheep track to guide you through the mess.

(I shall never again denigrate sheep's intelligence. Trust sheep. They know their stuff.)

Here, then, is what I advise. Think of the Thornaraigh River as a bow that bends to the south. What you want is to string that bow by walking on the river's north side, under Arnaval's shoulder, where the ground is firmer, the grass and heather are shorter, and there's an ATV track much of the way. To accomplish this, take the Mingarry footpath almost to its terminus at Loch an Caorach. That's about 20 minutes. (You can save time by driving down the path, but you won't save much, for you must do it very slowly.) You will come to a section where a portion of the loch spills over the path, forcing you to detour around the spill. There's a cleverly positioned wooden plank to help you. Do not, I repeat, do not, head straight for the Thornaraigh at this point, or you will encounter tussocks. That's another new word I learned: it describes tall clumps of grass surrounded by deep crevices. The clumps are unstable; when you walk on them you're like a circus elephant trying to balance itself on a huge rubber ball. The crevices fill up with water in the wet seasons. You wouldn't want to fall in. In the summer they're dry, except at the bottoms, but you still wouldn't want to fall in, for you could break an ankle or worse. Instead, head north until you find the track. Follow it east till you've passed Arnaval and Stulaval looms in front of you. You will have to cross the Thornaraigh twice, but there are stepping stones at both locations (though you'll require a stick and boots to traverse them safely). I went in the long way – via the south bank – and needed three hours and fifteen minutes to reach Stulaval's peak. I shaved fifty minutes off that time by stringing the bow on my return journey. The views from the peak, 374 metres above sea level – especially the views across Loch Aineort – are among the most spectacular on the island.

What about those other conquests I trumpeted? I said at the beginning that I have gathered enough material, on this visit, for several articles. They will carry me through December, when I plan to return and do more 'field research' in the hills.

The relevant map references are provided after article No. 3 ('Mist Connection').

25. *Summer Hillwalking – St. Kilda*

Iconic Village Bay on St. Kilda

MY older son visited the Pyramids earlier this summer. My wife Beth and I went one better: we visited St. Kilda. (St. Kilda is a dual UNESCO World Heritage Site, cultural and natural; the Pyramids, a cultural site only.) During our brief stay, I added Conachair – the archipelago's tallest eminence – to the 'conquests' I'd enumerated in last month's hill-walking article. That, however, was a mere incident to the pilgrimage.

I had read of these islands and seen photographs: of the cliffs, the now-derelict dwellings, and the hardy folk who once occupied those dwellings, their long dead eyes gazing into mine through the camera's medium. But I had never expected to go there. Though St. Kilda lies just forty miles west of the Uists, and is sometimes visible from Ben Mòr and Cleitreval, I had imagined it as I do Atlantis or Ultima Thule: unattainable and even fantastical.

That changed in July, thanks to my fellow-columnist Alasdair MacEachen, who knows St. Kilda intimately. He organized a day trip for a small party of close relatives – his mother, Katie, going for the first time; his sister Angela, a noted Gaelic-language broadcaster; and his 15-year-old nephew Allan – and friends. Having shepherded my family and me to Wiay last December (as reported in these pages), Alasdair judged us fit enough to be invited along. Our boys were unavailable – Max was bound for the Pyramids, and Adam remained in Connecticut – but Beth and I accepted eagerly.

Rising early, we drove an hour-and-a-half to the old harbour at Berneray. The 'Kilda Cruises' boat *Orca II*, operated by owner Angus Campbell and his helper, Chris, was standing by for an 8 am departure. Some two hours later St. Kilda appeared mirage-like in the distance, its cliffs half hidden in mist. I welcomed that mist, for it lent a spectral aura to the place – as if the islands were looming up, not only from the sea, but also from the past, and we were beholding them through a time warp. We anchored off the largest island, Hirta, and the boat's dinghy ferried us ashore.

St. Kilda's native inhabitants, who all lived on Hirta, departed forever in 1930. But researchers occupy some of their former cottages, although not permanently: they are rotated in and out every few weeks. One of them welcomed us and gave a short safety lecture. After that, we separated into two groups. The larger, including Beth, explored the old settlement, known as 'the Village,' under the leadership of John Love of Snishival, a member of our party and also a world-renowned biologist and author. (His book, 'A Natural History of St. Kilda,' is a definitive study of the indigenous wildlife.) The other headed for Conachair. Of course I joined that one, as did Alasdair, its guide; Billy MacPhee of Hebridean Jewellery (a talented accordionist who treated us to a concert on the return boat ride, accompanied by Allan on the drums); and Billy's partner, nurse Joan MacDonald.

We began by mounting the Gap, a high plateau, so-called because it separates Conachair from nearby Oiseval, another hill. But it deserves its name for a second reason: there is nothing beyond it but a sheer cliff drop to the sea. Steering respectfully clear of the rim, we followed the cliff line toward Conachair.

Conachair is 1411 feet high, if you trust online encyclopedias, or 1398 feet if you believe Alasdair and Angus. (I do.) Regardless, it is taller than any Uists hill except the big three: Mòr, Corrodale, Hecla. Moreover, the angle of ascent is steep, the grass that day was wet, and I cursed myself unceasingly for forgetting my walking stick. At first we despaired of reaching our goal, for clouds veiled the summit, but as we probed cautiously below them, parallel to the ridge, they lifted momentarily and we scrambled up. The photo I took shows only the cairn, partly because of the clouds and partly because the one other feature is the cliff edge immediately behind it. As the saying goes, the first step is the worst.

We descended via the military road and roamed the village, where we communed with ghosts. I could not initially credit that the MoD had considered bulldozing these relics. But then I read George Brown's 'Beside the Ocean of Time,' and I credit it now. Thankfully the project was aborted.

An unexpected thrill (additional to the concert) awaited us on the return voyage: the boat detoured directly beneath the cliffs. Thousands of seabirds blanketed the rock-faces, making them as white as Dover's. I wanted to stare upward in wide-eyed and open-mouthed wonder. Wisely, I resisted.

Mythical Brigadoon is accessible only once a century. The same may prove true for me of St. Kilda. But at least mine eyes have seen its glory.

There seems little purpose to my providing map references for St. Kilda, for one does not walk to it. I suggest that interested readers contact either 'Kilda Cruises' or any of the other companies that offer a boat service.

26. *Loch Stulaval, Truirebheinn, Ben Kenneth*

The beach at Loch Stulaval

MY ORIGINAL plan that warm July day was simple. I would mostly replicate a winter walk that I had described in the February 2008 issue. I would begin at the more westerly of the two pedestrian causeways near Lasgair. (I prefer it to the other because you can drive right up to it and leave your car there.) Then, in succession: northeast from the causeway to Diollaid Pass on Triuirebheinn's northern shoulder. The Pass down to Loch nan Arm. Southeast, first along the loch's western shore and next through a nameless pass into the stark eastern glens that lie in Triuirebheinn's shadow. South through the glens. From one of them, Nostapal, west up to Triuirebheinn's southern shoulder and north to its peak, 1161 feet high but easily accessible from the shoulder. I had done it all before.

I contemplated only one variation. Because the summer days are much longer than winter ones, I hoped to descend afterwards into Coire na Cuilc, the rugged pass between Triuirebheinn and its southern neighbour Ben Kenneth, and then climb Kenneth, which is 919 feet tall. I had done that too, but separately, and not in a while.

I started at 11.20. I was equipped as usual: hiking boots, to keep my feet dry; a walking stick; one water bottle (I could have used more – but loch water is potable); light snacks; and a cap that I mostly didn't wear because I found it uncomfortable. Instead I used suntan lotion, which was a mistake, for the stuff burnt my eyes. The first leg of the walk, to Diollaid, was unremarkable: the terrain was undulating but monotonous, with no striking features; moreover, the houses of Lochboisdale, Lasgair and Daliburgh were clearly visible at my back, depriving me of the wondrous sense of solitude that helps make hillwalking appealing. An hour and forty minutes of steady trudging brought me to Diollaid's base. Then my plan changed.

Beyond Diollaid, and separating it from Loch Stulaval, stands a group of small hills, leading down to the loch, which the Ordnance Survey calls 'Cleit' (in English, 'rocky outcrop'). I remembered at that point that Diollaid, with its thick, high heather, had been a slow and arduous proposition even in December and was likely to be worse in July. I also reminded myself that I had never explored 'Cleit.' So I opted to try it now.

Next to proposing to my wife and building my Locheynort cottage, it was my best decision ever. The ascents and descents were gentle, and the vistas that opened up ahead – Loch Stulaval's secluded eastern extremity below me, Stulaval looming across and above it to the north, glens and foothills on my right – were among the most magnificent I've beheld anywhere. I strolled down to a sand beach on the loch's southeastern shore and, knowing myself to be completely alone, cooled off by taking a quick swim. The only onlookers, sheep, averted their eyes in modesty. Or in horror.

Refreshed, I approached Loch nan Arm from the northwest – much easier than going via Diollaid – and, skirting its eastern rather than western edge, continued through the nameless pass into the eastern glens, where I found solitude aplenty. I was reassured, during the sometimes difficult passage, by the recurring sight of human footprints; whether they were mine, from two winters ago, or another person's, they meant that someone had taken this identical route and returned safely (or so I supposed, since I'd not heard of any recent hillwalking calamities). The climb up Triuirebheinn was uneventful. I made sure to keep it so by avoiding a well-remembered bog, the largest I've seen, just below the shoulder. My stick could not touch bottom.

As I felt my way down to Coire na Cuilc, I had to decide whether to climb Ben Kenneth. I concluded that I shouldn't, for I was thirsty and out of water, with no lochs in view, and my boots were pinching badly. So of course I did. Alas, by the time I committed myself I had left the easiest route, from the north, far behind. Instead I hoisted myself up what seemed an almost sheer slope, which fortunately had lots of ledges, handholds and footholds. Scrambling over repeated false summits, I finally reached the true top at around 5.30. Thence I returned to my car – after first phoning my friend Mike Mason, who owns the easternmost house at Lasgair and who took a photo of me from below to help me prove my conquest in case I'm challenged.

The round-trip distance was perhaps six miles, the total walking time (including the swim) just under eight hours. If you do it in summer, bring more water than I did. And a bathing costume, to spare the sensibilities of the sheep.

Loch Stulabhal (Stuleval) is located at NGR NF 800 230, although it also extends considerably east, west and south of there; its eastern end, at which I went swimming, is nearer to NGR NF 810. Cleit is located slightly northwest of NGR NF 810 220. The map references for Truirebheinn are provided after article No. 8 ('Truirebheinn and the Eastern Glens'). Beinn Ruigh Choinnich (Ben Kenneth) is located immediately northwest of NGR NF 810 190; its western base extends as far as NGR NF 800.

27. *Miscellany*

The beach track and causeway leading to Orasay Island

I told readers last August that I had done enough walking, during my previous month's stay, to write several articles. That was no exaggeration, for this will be the fourth. In it, I shall first recount my visits to a trio of mid-sized hills that stand in or closely adjacent to the Mingarry valley: Shurabhat (150 metres), Aisgerbheinn (126 metres) and Leathabhal (182 metres). I shall also describe some new path walks.

Shurabhat is at the valley's southeastern edge. To get there, start out as if you were going to Stulabhal: walk almost to the end of the Mingarry footpath and turn north at the spillway that crosses the path from Loch nan Caorach. (You can also drive down the path, but do it slowly!) Continue north a short way till you come to an ATV track, then follow the track in a southeasterly direction across the Thornaraigh River (there are stepping stones) to Arnabhal's southern shoulder. Shurabhat will be at your right on the far side of the valley. You will pass Loch Shurabhat on your left as you cross over. The climb is gentle, for Shurabhat is unusual in having no false summits: what you see is what you get. And what you see, from the top, are remarkable views of Stulabhal and Loch Snigiscleit to the far northwest. The walk is only about half as long as to Stulabhal – two-and-a-half miles, one-and-a-half hours each way (minus about twenty minutes each way if you do the path by auto) – and the scenery is almost as rewarding.

Leathabhal (in English, Layaval) closes off the southern end of the Mingarry valley. The easiest access, though, is not through the valley but from neighbouring Aisgerbheinn (Askerveinn). Accordingly, I shall discuss three destinations together: the Aisgerbheinn path towards Aisgerbheinn's summit; Aisgerbheinn; and finally, Leathabhal itself.

As Holmes famously remarked to Watson, 'You see, but you do not observe.' Though I must have driven past it hundreds of times, I had never noticed the track that curves eastward up Aisgerbheinn from the A865, kitty corner across from the Askernish Road, to the television tower near the summit. Paved in part, after a fashion, it can carry ATVs (or so I'm told), but not ordinary vehicles. During my summer visit I noticed it at last, and of course felt impelled to explore it. A brisk 20-minute walk up a steep incline brought me to the tower; from there a narrow trail leads to the summit, a short distance away. There is a cairn at the summit, and a small flagpole rises, incongruously, from its top, still bearing the remnants of some unrecognizable flag. (Can any reader explain that flag?)

If you're feeling more adventurous, you can proceed as I did from Aisgerbheinn to Leathabhal. The best way to accomplish this is to leave the track when you are directly opposite Leathabhal's closest point. This will be at a sharp bend where the tower first comes into full view. The summit is now forty minutes away, almost due east, across a narrow valley bisected by the Bharp River. (In summer, anyhow, the 'river' is but a sluggish stream, and you can step over it easily.) A cautionary note: there are numerous false summits – ten from the time I started counting – but you will know when you've found the true one. After feeling my way through a cloud, I shared that summit briefly with a full-antlered buck until he, scorning my company, scuttled off toward Stulabhal. You will not see Loch Snigiscleit from here, but you will enjoy rewarding vistas of the Mingarry valley and the adjoining hills.

As for the path walks, I shall mention two. The first is a magnificent almost mile-long trail that hugs the beach from the campground at the end of the Garrynamonie Road to the tidal island of Orasay. If the tides are right (be sure to ascertain them beforehand) you can cross an isthmus to the island itself. It contains two adjacent hillocks, which, though small, are steep enough to provide exercise. The eastern views, stunning ones, are of South Uist's beaches both north and south. The western view is of Boston.

Finally, I fulfilled a long-time ambition by locating the source of the gamekeeper's ATV track to Corodale. The track begins just below Loch Olaidh an Ear, off the A865, next to a structure that appears to be a fishing station. From there to Corodale is about five miles. One needn't complete the entire route, but at least cross what the ordnance map (incorrectly) calls the 'Beanna Beag' Pass into the valley beneath Beinn Mhòr, where a chain of lochs stretches out ahead of you. Wow.

I have not finished capitalising on those walks that I took last summer. Stay tuned.

Shurabhat (Shuravat) stretches diagonally, northwest to southeast, from NGR NF 780 240 to NGR NF 790 230. Aisgerbheinn (Askerveinn) also stretches diagonally northwest to southeast: from NGR NF 750 240 to NGR NF 760 230. Leathabhal (Layaval) extends northwards between NGR NF 770 230 and NGR NF 780 230. The map references for Loch Olaidh an Ear are provided after article No. 20 ('The Gamekeeper's Track to Corodale'). You can pick up the beach path at any of a number of places – since writing the article I have learned that it runs all the way south to South Smerclate – but the place where I joined it, the Gearraidh na Monadh (Garrynamonie) campground, is located almost midway between NGR NF 740 160 and NGR NF 740 170: nearer to the former.

28. *Eaval*

Eaval from the beach at Loch Obasaraigh

VIEWED from the west, North Uist's Eaval is a sucker punch. (You know the metaphor: the seemingly friendly handshake, followed suddenly by the unexpected wrenching blow to the gut.) It appears to slope upward, south to north, at an even, gentle angle, much like a bicycle ramp. The jaunt, you'd think, could scarcely tire you, and if it did, why, once having attained the 347-metre-high summit, you could simply roll back downhill to the base.

Wrong. There is only one western approach to Eaval, from Claddach Chairinis over two miles of mostly spongy ground and across a narrow isthmus. While the journey has attractions, including a magnificent hidden lake fort, it's a slog. Then, as you near the base, two miles from your starting point, the sucker punch awaits: the gentle ramp dissolves into four or five separate hills, each higher than its predecessor, and you must go up and down at least three of them to reach the top. (Sorry to be imprecise, but it's years since I climbed Eaval from this direction.) You'll curse them all before you finish.

There is, however, another way, from the north. I discovered it only last summer. (I've said that these islands always hold surprises.) It's faster: four-and-a-half hours in total, compared to six if you start at Claddach Chairinis. It's easier, for it is the one hill on the archipelago that has a path all the way to the top – well, almost to the top; the path disappears in places as you get close, but by that time you can find your own way up. Although the final ascent is steep, it's the only serious obstacle that you face: those pesky foothills are on the far, that is, the southern side of the peak. And the walk is stunningly beautiful – I would say the most beautiful I've taken, except that I feel that way about almost every walk here while I'm taking it. It's fortunate for my marriage that I don't feel the same about women.

To get there, turn east off the A867 onto the B894, also called the Loch Euphort Road, just south of Barpa Langass. Follow that road to the end, at Obisary, and leave your car next to a shed; there's ample parking space. Walk due east, through a stile, past the last house, which will be on your left. Beyond it lies a meadow. Pick your way through the meadow carefully, for nobody cleans up after its numerous sheep. But if you persevere you will soon find the path. Almost immediately afterward you will reach a wide river, bridged by stepping-stones. If the stones are flooded, as I'm told they can be, the river is impassable, but I took the walk twice and had no problems. The path resumes on the far side. Hugging Loch Obasaraigh, it thereafter extends, almost without interruption, to Eaval's base and then up the mountain's northern slope, passing under oddly-shaped Burrabhal (140 metres) – which seemed well worth a detour, but I kept going – and curving south around a sparkling beach at the loch's eastern extremity. Bring your camera.

If you're hillwalking-averse, as my wife is, don't bother to climb; just follow the path as far as the fancy takes you. That alone is memorable.

I have not exhausted the subject of last summer's walks, for I've yet to describe Easabhal. To do that, I shall have to check some reference points on my next visit, which will begin about when this newspaper hits the shops. And I also climbed Mhòr, four times, but I have made Mhòr the subject of several past articles, so why repeat? On one of those climbs, I set off from the water station near the A865. To my dismay, I needed two hours to reach the summit, whereas a previous walk from that direction had taken only an hour-and-a-half. Perhaps it was because the hill was ten years younger then and had not attained its full height.

About times and distances: I walk slowly, as suits my years and would suit my dignity had I dignity to suit. My sons need less time because they walk faster (though I worry lest in consequence they step into a crevice, break an ankle, and return by helicopter). As for distances, I rely on my ordnance map and a ruler. I've made mistakes, but GPS systems are not foolproof either. Last July a friend used a GPS to check my measurements of the distance from Mingarry to Stulaval. I'd estimated four miles; the GPS said 2.38.

I was astonished: could I have been that wrong? We looked again, and lo, the GPS had confused Stuleval with Trinival. Transposing Stuleval to its proper place, we re-measured: 4.03 miles. John Henry had bested the machine, and lived to boast.

Author's Postscript: Since this article was written, the shed at the beginning of the Eaval footpath has been transformed into an attractive craft shop. And I have climbed Burrabhal, which is indeed well worth the detour if time and daylight allow.

Eabhal's (Eaval's) summit is located at approximately NGR NF 820 330 on OS Explorer no. 454.

29. *Spin and Beinn Mhòr*

Spin, and behind it, Beinn Mhòr from the dam at Loch Iarris

TAKING advantage of unseasonably balmy temperatures (which soon plummeted), I enjoyed excellent walking after arriving on the islands during the second week of December. I didn't climb 620-metre-high Beinn Mhòr when I wanted to climb it, but did climb it when I didn't want to climb it. In the course of the failed attempt, I discovered an intriguing new destination.

Here was my initial plan. I would depart for Mhòr from the gamekeeper's ATV track that begins at Loch Olaidh an Ear's fishing station, about a quarter-mile above the Loch

Aineort Road. (The track, which extends for five miles all the way into Glen Corrodale, is itself a worthwhile venture.) Crossing over the second, that is, the stone footbridge, I would follow the track east as far as Beinn Bheag Tuath ('Little North Hill'), then strike out northeast over open country till I reached Mhòr's peak. Since I imagined in my hubris that I knew the terrain well, I did not bother consulting an ordnance map.

That was dumb. Had I done so, I would have realized that an obstacle stood in my way, concealed behind a ridge. The obstacle was Loch Iarris: a huge, jagged, spectacularly beautiful interior loch (artificial, it seems, for a dam encloses it), which feeds the water supply. By the time I circled around its eastern shore, I dared not continue to Mhòr in the scant remaining daylight, tantalisingly close though its peak appeared. So I scrambled instead up an odd-looking hump on the far side of the loch, just below where Mhòr swings north and starts to slope downward. That suited me well enough, for the hump's summit, crowned by a cairn, afforded excellent views across Loch Aineort and over the machair to the ocean.

I later learned that the hump has a name: Spin (the meaning of which I have been unable to ascertain). And it is a worthy objective in its own right. At 356 metres – one less than Truirebheinn – it is the sixth tallest hill on the Uists: one of just seven that exceed a thousand feet. It took me two-and-a-half hours to get there and two to get back. The reason the return journey was shorter was that this time I skirted Loch Iarris to the west – a more direct route – and, eschewing the ATV track, reached the fishing station via a wooden footbridge that brought me almost to my car. I could probably have done it faster in drier seasons, but the ground (which is difficult in the best of conditions; the September issue of Trail Magazine describes it as possibly 'the roughest in Britain') was exceptionally wet from recent rains. I was fortunate to have worn boots.

A few days later my friend Dave, from the Isle of Man, joined me for two days of walking. On the first day, I brought him to Spin; for good measure we returned over Beinn Bheag Tuath, which at 170 metres, including several false summits, is not without its challenges. The next day, we decided to take things easier. Leaving our car at the North Loch Aineort turnabout, we would join the gamekeeper's track at approximately its midpoint, just below Beinn Mhòr, and walk east along the track until it angled north towards Corrodale. We would then reverse direction and head home.

At first all went smoothly. The track brought us past Mhòr, past Bealach Crosgard ('Crosgard Pass'), which separates Mhòr from Beinn nan Caorach, then past Beinn nan Caorach itself. But when we reached the latter's base, at the entrance to yet another pass, Dave looked at me and said, "Marty." I knew what was coming, for I've walked with him often: he wanted to double back over Beinn nan Caorach – which looked so invitingly gentle – and tackle Mhòr from the east. I wanted no such thing, but he was my guest, so I obliged.

It wasn't gentle, of course, and we made it harder than necessary by walking directly over instead of around Beinn nan Caorach's crest. But we found a sort of natural path, at Crosgard's southern mouth, which brought us part way up Mhòr's shoulder. We arrived at the trig point at 1 pm, three hours and ten minutes after setting out, surprisingly encountering no wind even at the top. That left us enough time – barely – to get back to our car before sunset.

In previous years I'd outpaced Dave, despite his being younger than I am, but on this visit I struggled to keep up with him. That's okay, for it is not a competition: the only competition is between body and spirit, and the trick is to get the latter to accept the limitations of the former as I approach my eighth decade.

Spin extends northwards between NGR NF 790 310 and NGR NF 800 310. Loch Iarris is located midway between NGR NF 780 310 and NGR NF 790 310, immediately south of the 310 coordinate. Beinn Bheag Tuath (Little North Hill) extends northwards between NGR NF 780 300 and NGR NF 790 300. Beinn nan Caorach (Hill of the Sheep) is located at NGR NF 820 290; it stretches northwest and southeast from there. Other relevant map references have been provided after previous articles.

30. *Easabhal, Kenneth, Sunamul*

Max and Adam atop Ben Kenneth in winter

I REPORTED last month on the good use I'd made of the balmy mid-December weather that warmed these islands before the snows hit: discovering Spin, and taking a circuitous hike that culminated, unexpectedly, on top of Beinn Mhòr. Those were the longest treks of my winter visit. But I also completed others which, though shorter, were equally satisfying.

For one, my older son Max and I lured my wife Beth – a most reluctant hillwalker – up Easabhal, on South Uist's southwestern corner. Easabhal is an excellent 'starter' hill if you do it the right way. At 243 metres (797 feet) it is taller than its neighbours – it is indeed the highest eminence below Lochboisdale – but it is near the road, and the ascents are short, gentle and separated by long stretches of fairly level plateau, so that the novice climber (Beth, for instance) has ample opportunity to pause and recuperate. And the top, instead of tapering off into a conical peak like most Uist hills, is itself a plateau that the walker can explore at leisure. Since the adjacent hills are smaller, there are excellent views in all directions.

What is the right way? Let me first rule out the wrong ones. Do not approach Easabhal from the east – that is, from the terminus of the South Glendale Road – because the terrain is boggy, there are several barbed wire fences, and you face a stiff climb.

A western approach, off the B888, initially seems more promising: when you come to the Garrynamonie Road on your right, a long footpath extends opposite it almost to Easabhal's northern shoulder. However, there is wisdom in the saying that if something seems too good to be true, it probably is. The walk proceeds smoothly until the path ends, but thereafter one must veer obliquely left in order to join the hill at its base, and the intervening ground is nasty. It has taken me an hour to reach the top from this direction.

No: the easiest way up is from the beginning of the South Glendale Road. Drive past the Eriskay causeway, and then past the first house on your right, which sits just beyond a cattle grid. After another hundred yards or so, you will see, on your left, a rough track, wide enough for cars, that leads to what looks like an abandoned quarry below a radio tower. Turn into the track, park (there's room), climb towards the tower, and then follow the natural contours of the landscape to the top. Be sure to keep to the near, that is, the south side of a deep crevice that divides the foothills. With Beth in tow, the walk took almost an hour each way – there are three or four false summits – but I have done it alone in about 45 minutes. Beth enjoyed it, mostly, but doubts that she'll replicate it anytime soon.

The two boys and I also climbed Ben Kenneth after the snows fell: a very different proposition from doing it in the summer. We took the Lasgair footbridge, scrambled over a low ridge on our right, and made it to the peak in an hour-and-a-half. We were rewarded by spectacular white vistas across the Mingarry valley, as well as southward toward Barra.

The highlight of our visit, though, was a pilgrimage by all four of us to the tidal island of Sunamul, off Benbecula: scarcely a hillwalk, as the terrain is table-top flat, but taxing nevertheless, for the weather was cold and the ground was spongy. We are indebted for the experience to Alasdair Maceachen, who acted as our Virgil, as he had done previously in bringing us to Wiay and St. Kilda. We'd have been hard put to find Sunamul on our own: indeed, all I can say even now is that the route begins near the Benbecula golf course and runs, for a time, parallel to the airport (one cannot go when planes are taking off or landing) before crossing a wide estuary.

Alasdair has a special connection to the place, because his mother's people were its last resident family. The island is beautiful and haunting, and there is no finer prospect in these parts than that of distant Eaval. If you venture there on your own, just remember to check the tides first. And the plane schedules.

As a bonus, Alasdair brought us afterwards to the hidden ruins of a little-known chapel, the Cill in Balivanich, one of the Uists' oldest structures, on the far side of the B892. You'll need tall boots to get to it, for it is accessible only across marshes. But it's worth the effort.

This newspaper's next issue is due 4th March – the day I'm to arrive here again in quest of new adventures. Stay tuned.

❖

I have provided map references for Easaval after article No. 9 ('Winter Walks') and for Ben Kenneth after article No. 26 ('Loch Stuleval, Triurebheinn, Ben Kenneth'). Sunamul is located between NGR NF 800 570 and NGR NF 810 570.

31. *March Meanderings*

Stuleval, from Arneval's peak, on the day I walked them both

THE WEATHER throughout my recent visit was unseasonably balmy – eight days of almost uninterrupted sunshine, unprecedented in March – and I roamed the hills on every one of them. I'll recount my adventures in diary form, pausing when I run out of space and resuming next month.

Thursday, 4 March: this was my first full day here, and I started slowly, with a morning walk up Beinn Bheag Deas. Little South Hill, to use its English name, is just behind my North Locheynort cottage. The ordnance map does not give its height, but it seems about the same size as its neighbour, Little North Hill. That would make it approximately 170 metres: a brisk climb, but not too taxing. The easiest way up is via a patch of clear ground, green with rock flooring, opposite a pair of vacant bothies on the far side of the road. The cleared area ends abruptly, giving way to heather. From that point, continue at a slightly rightward tilt to a gate in a barbed wire fence. If you can't find the gate, don't worry: several sections of barbed wire are missing on the hill's western shoulder – left as you ascend – so you can cross the fence comfortably there as well. Once you're through it, the rest is easy. Though the summit is not especially high, it rates a cairn, and affords superb vistas: Loch Eynort and Meall Mhòr to the east; Beinn Mhòr and its loch-studded valley to the north. I toyed with carrying on across the valley to Spin, or perhaps to Mhòr itself, but the skies for the moment looked threatening. So I scrambled down the hill's northern slope, and, following the new footpaths and public footpath, circled back through the forest to my starting point. The outing consumed less than an hour.

The threatening skies having cleared, I later took the Aisgerbheinn footpath, off the main road, past the television tower to the top, 126 metres above sea level. ('Footpath' is a misnomer, for the track can supposedly accommodate all-wheel drive vehicles, but I wouldn't risk my car.) Thence, replicating a walk I'd done last July – see the November '09 issue – I crossed the Bharp River valley to Layaval (182 metres), or, as I call it, Layaval-of-the-Many-False-Summits. In July I'd counted ten of those; now there were fewer, but this was because I approached from a more southerly direction. Instead of the lone stag that had briefly joined me the last time, I passed a herd of eight, all with full antlers. I could have reached Layaval in an hour if I'd gone directly, which would have meant abandoning the track where it curves back towards the tower and striking out east across the valley. By exploring Aigerbheinn, however, I added a half-hour to the journey. From Layaval back to my car was an hour exactly. Both hills offer birds-eye views of the island's centre.

Friday, 5 March: I waxed more ambitious, proceeding first from the Mingarry footpath to Stuleval (374 metres) and then over Arneval (257 metres) on the homeward leg. I excised a mile each way from the eight-mile (round-trip) trek by driving up the footpath almost to the end, till I found room to park. If you do likewise, drive slowly: eight miles per hour max. Because I've described this route before, I'll be brief. Whether you walk or drive down the footpath, leave it where Loch nan Caorach's spill-off courses over it, and turn north till you come to an ATV track. Follow the track east. It crosses the Thornaraigh River twice, much as a string connects the two ends of a bow, the river being the bow. The second crossing deposits you almost at Stuleval. The first (western) crossing is nasty – the stepping stones are loose, and you'll need boots and a stick – but if you avoid the crossings by staying south of the river you'll find that its bend diverts you over rough terrain. The nearly-taut 'bowstring' passes directly beneath Arnaval's southern shoulder.

Returning, I created unnecessary complications by descending south from Stuleval, through a narrow pass, before heading west. In consequence I had to negotiate a formidable field of tussocks. Luckily the ground was dry. However, it was full of ticks that I plucked off myself in droves that evening. I also experienced some scary moments when the setting sun, shining in my face, blotted out familiar landmarks. But the track always loomed below or in front of me: a scar on the landscape, as critics rightly complain, yet all the more visible and useful for that, and I found my car before dark. My travel time: two-and-a-half hours to Stuleval, three-and-a-half back over Arneval. The views from Stuleval are among the Uists' finest.

The best is still coming.

Author's Postscript: I have since ascertained that my guess as to Little South Hill's height was close to the mark: the hill is 167 metres tall, just three less than its northern neighbour.

Beinn Bheag Deas's (Little South Hill's) summit is located slightly southwest of NGR NF 790 290. Airneabhal (Arneval) occupies the area between NGR NF 780 260 and NGR NF 790 250. Other relevant map references are provided after previous articles.

32. Beinn Tairbeirt to the Flood Gate

*From Beinn Tairbeirt's peak to Hecla; Loch Spotal is faintly
visible at the far left*

EVERYONE has heard of 'Munros': Scottish mountains,
3000 feet or more above sea level, which are named for
the hardy adventurer who first summitted all of them a
century ago. Scotland also boasts 'Corbetts' (2500–2599 feet),
'Grahams' (2000–2499 feet), and 'Marilyns,' which are
measured in relation to the tallest adjacent eminence rather
than to the sea. The Uists have an abundance of Marilyns,
but only one Graham – Beinn Mhòr – and no Corbetts or
Munros.

I have coined a name for a different set of hills: 'Beths', in honour of my wife. These are hills that seem tailor-made for reluctant climbers like... Beth. They are what I have elsewhere called 'starter' hills: below 800 feet, close to the roads, and with gentle ascents. Ruabhal (Rueval), on Benbecula, is a Beth, as are Easabhal (Easaval), Aisgerbheinn (Askervein) and Beinn Bheag Deas (Little South Hill) on South Uist. In contrast, Seabhal (Sheaval) and Trinneabhal (Trinival), at South Locheynort, are not Beths. Though qualifying in some respects, they are steep and boggy, and their namesake would not enjoy them.

Beinn Tairbeirt (Ben Tarbert – in English, 'isthmus'), on the north side of the Sgiopoirt (Skipport) Road, is a Beth by every criterion. It is 546 feet high, a short distance from the road, and an easy climb if you approach it right.

And so on Saturday, 6th March, the third full day of my recent March stay (I'd promised in the April issue to keep recounting my March adventures in diary form), I drove to the fourth marked passing place after the Sgiopoirt Road forest, just beyond Loch Airigh na h-Achiais. Coming from the west, the marker and loch are on the left, the passing place on the right. I left the car next to the passing area, with room for other drivers to use it as intended, and headed for the top. Beth was not with me – she was home in the States – so this was a scouting expedition in anticipation of her next visit. Because I was alone, my plans were more ambitious than if she had accompanied me: Beinn Tairbeirt was not an end in itself, but merely a means to an end; my ultimate objective was the Flood Gate, which connects Loch Sgiopoirt with Loch Bi (Bee). This geological wonder, slightly above a mile from my starting point, has always impressed me as the most beautiful spot on these islands – except when I'm savouring some other local marvel.

There are two ways of getting to the Flood Gate and Beinn Tairbeirt, and I've described both before. One is from the Sgiopoirt Road. The other, a tad longer, is from the opposite direction: beginning at the East Gerinish end of the Loch Charnain (Carnan) road, take the footpath that commences just beyond the last house. When the path forks, follow the right fork past a ruined schoolhouse and continue along the path (it peters out in places) to the Flood Gate. If you want to go to the Flood Gate but not the hill, this is how to do it; it is a fairly level stroll of perhaps an hour each way. If, on the other hand, you're aiming for the hill but not the Flood Gate, you start from the Sgiopoirt side. My sights were on both.

Skirting Loch Airaig na h-Aichias's eastern shore, I circled west, where the ascent was smoother. The obelisk at the top was visible from the road. It vanished as I started to climb, but reappeared when I was halfway up. It took me just half an hour to reach it. I could have gotten there even sooner, but I was still aching from the previous day's two-peak coup (Stulabhal, Airneabhal; see previous article) and in consequence proceeded slowly. From Tairbeirt's summit you can see, among Thacla's (Hecla's) foothills, sparkling interior lochs – Spotail; Fada – that are otherwise hidden.

Getting up was no trouble, but the descent down Tairbeirt's northern slope toward the Flood Gate, and the re-ascent on the way back, were a different story: precipitous, through thick heather, with crevices underneath – not Beth's cup of tea. Though the distances from the road to the peak and the peak to the Flood Gate are about the same, I needed an hour and ten minutes to negotiate the latter.

You can cross the Flood Gate over either a metal footbridge or a stone-and-earth dam. The two stand side-by-side. Shun the bridge unless you've a head for heights, for it is narrow and slippery, and lacks railings. The dam is blocked by a fence, but you can climb it comfortably. Are the views worth the slog? See the accompanying photo. And stay tuned for days four through eight.

Author's Postscript: Since this article was written, Beth has accompanied me up Beinn Tairbeirt, under snow cover no less. And (mostly) enjoyed it.

Loch Airigh na h-Achais is located immediately southwest of NGR NF 810 390. Other relevant map references are provided after article No. 6 ('The Flood Gate to Ben Tarbert').

33. *Coire na Cuilc and East Coast*

The cave at Coire na Cuilc

My diary of my March visit continues.

DAY FOUR: I resolved to do something new, which is not easy for me, as I believe that I have uncovered nearly all of the island's topographical secrets. For instance, I had been many times to Coire na Cuilc (Corrie of the Reeds), which lies between Truirebheinn and Beinn Ruigh Choinnich (Ben Kenneth). And, each time, I had looked up in awe at the spectacular cave that penetrates the coire's northeastern rock face. In its recesses, so local legend goes, Prince Charles

Edward Stuart, Neil MacEachen of Tobha Beag (Howbeg), and Captain Felix O'Neil of the Irish Brigade had first met to plan the Great Escape.

But I had never actually climbed to the cave, much less gone inside. For one thing, it is difficult to reach: you must either scramble up to it almost vertically, using handholds and footholds to avoid falling several yards to the ground, or creep along a narrow ledge to the right of the entrance. For another – and to me, more dauntingly – the entrance had always been guarded by those staples of west highland and island landscape: decomposing sheep carcasses. I was too squeamish to dispute the passage with these sentinels. Nor had I ever proceeded from Coire na Cuilc all the way to Rubha na Creige Moire on the east coast. I decided that this time I would enter the cave, unless the sentinels were still at their posts, and, after exploring it, continue on to the Minch. I was also open to possibly climbing Beinn Choinnich from the north, a direction I had not previously attempted, on my way back.

I set out, ten minutes before noon, from the pedestrian causeway at Lasgair. This is the easternmost of the three causeways that span the channel connecting Loch Baghasdail (Boisdale) to Loch a Bharp – hence, the closest to my objectives. From there I followed an ATV track that brought me to the dam at Loch nan Smalag. I skirted the loch to the north (the south side would have done just as well) and reached the cave shortly after one. This leg of the journey covered two miles of mostly level terrain.

Scrutinising the opening from below, I ascertained that the grim sentinels of yore had vanished. So I climbed to the ledge, crawled along it till I reached the aperture, and peered inside. No dead sheep immediately confronted me, but there was evidence that plenty of live ones had visited recently, and, at the cave's terminus, perhaps twenty yards in, I saw a cleanly picked sheep skeleton. My curiosity satisfied, indeed quenched, by these twin discoveries, I penetrated no further. I am ever mistrustful of mutton.

Returning to ground level, I resumed my journey eastward, using sheep tracks to avoid the tall heather. Thanks to my wooly predecessors, I moved quickly, and arrived at the coast – perhaps a mile from the cave – at 2.20. The coast contains some truly dramatic rock formations, but they were slippery, and were pierced at one point by a crevice, of no small dimensions, which, had I tumbled into it, would have provided an unwelcome and probably one-way shortcut to the water. Feeling my way gingerly, I explored the area for some twenty minutes and then started back.

As I passed Beinn Choinnich on my left, I decided, reluctantly, against scaling it: I didn't trust the daylight, or my legs, and besides we had seen plenty of one another on previous visits. Instead, I exited the Coire just below Choinnich's northwestern shoulder – and gazed directly into the setting sun.

That sun blinded me, and, for a scary moment, disoriented me. I could make out Aisgerbheinn (Askerveinn) and Leathabhal (Layaval) in the distance, but were they where they belonged, relative to my position? Taking a deep breath, and consulting my compass, I reassured myself that they were. (It didn't help that I was tired and had run out of water.) I carried on cautiously, using those hills as guideposts. The ATV track was nowhere to be found; with the sun's rays in my eyes, I don't think I would have noticed it if I'd been standing on it. It was comforting indeed to see, at last, the houses of Lasgair before the daylight faded.

For all that I had walked this area many times before, I found myself, to my chagrin, well east of where I'd wanted to be when those houses finally appeared. I did not return to my car until 5.10 – a half-hour later than I'd planned, and only about a half-hour before sunset. A good thing I'd bypassed Choinnich! It was a salutary lesson on the dangers of complacency.

◈

Coire na Cuilc (Corrie of the Reeds) is located midway between NGR NF 810 200 and NGR NF 810 210; at least, that is the approximate point where one enters it. It extends eastwards from there. Rubha na Creige Moire is located slightly north of NGR NF 830 200.

34. *March Miscellany*

Looking north from Beinn Mhòr's summit at Corodale and Hecla

This article continues and concludes my running diary of my recent March adventures.

DAY FIVE: I spent most of the day visiting friends on Benbecula. To keep in shape, though, I took time off to walk Benbecula's Rueval footpath till it forks: the north fork leading to Roisinis (Rossinish), the south fork to Bagh Scaraloid (Scaraloid Bay) on Loch Uisgebhagh. The fork is about two miles from the A865, but one can drive the first quarter-mile, more or less, till one passes the skip on the left.

The scenery improves exponentially from there, with lochs and broad vistas in every direction. The path was relatively dry and the terrain is level, unless you detour over Rueval, which on this occasion I didn't; accordingly, I was able to negotiate the entire distance, coming and going, in less than an hour. I was tempted to pursue one track or the other to its terminus, as I have often done before – each is worth the effort – but it was getting late and I had more calls to make, so I desisted.

DAY SIX: For old time's sake, I returned to 606-metres-high Thacla (Hecla). I followed what has become my favourite route: from the Dreumasdal (Drimsdale) telephone station off the A865, down a short footpath to a sheepfold, then across open ground to Maoil Daimh and finally to the peak – approximately three miles, and two-and-a-half to three hours, in each direction. That's at my measured pace; my sons can do it faster.

Since I have described this walk in previous articles, I shall not go into detail, except to sound one cautionary note: on the return leg, passing over Na Creagan just beyond the aptly-named Loch nam Breac Ruadh (Loch of the Brown Trout), I took what I thought would be an easier way back. Instead of crossing Na Creagan at its highest point, directly ahead of me, I avoided the climb by veering right along the hill's gentle northern shoulder. That was what we call in the States a bush league – that is, a beginner's – mistake. Yes, I saved myself a few feet of altitude – but I emerged well north of the footpath and had to negotiate several undulating moors, all of them thick with heather, before locating it. I was lucky to reach it just before dark.

DAY SEVEN: I re-visited the now-familiar path that leads from Gleann Dail bho Tuath (North Glendale) to the deserted, ruined township at Thairteabagh (Hartaval Bay). My ultimate destination was Maol na-h'Ordaig, the oddly-shaped hump that overlooks the Minch about half an hour beyond the ruins: been there, done that, but I wanted to do it again.

The first part of the journey went smoothly. I drove from the B888 below Daliburgh down the North Glendale Road, turned south onto a short spur just before the end, left the car in a small parking space, and trudged east over wet ground and peaty foothills till I found the path. It brought me through the mournful, loch-studded glen past seemingly abandoned fish farms and over the stepping stones just south of Broken Bridge till I reached the ruins, two-and-a-half miles and one-and-a-quarter hours from my vehicle.

Alas, rain and blinding mist descended as I set out from there for the Maol, so I reluctantly turned back. I cursed my caution when the rain stopped and the mist lifted soon afterwards, but it was too late to retrace my steps. Still, seeing the ruins was satisfying enough.

DAY EIGHT (my last full day): I went – where else? – to Beinn Mhòr (Ben Mòr; Great Mountain), at 620 metres the monarch of the Uist hills, approaching it from the North Loch Aineort (Eynort) side: a distance of maybe two miles. I took my time: three-and-a-half hours out, three back. This direction offers many options. I chose to follow the public footpath almost to the end and, turning north, to circle around the eastern shore of Loch nam Faoileann (Loch of the Gulls). I then continued north across open country, past a deer fence immediately to my left, till I reached Bealach

Crosgard (Crosgard Pass), which separates Beinn Mhòr from its south-eastern neighbour Beinn nan Caorach (Hill of the Sheep). Would that I had artistry to paint the vistas from there over Airneabhal (Arnaval), on the far side of Loch Aineort, all the way south to Barra! From Crosgard to Mhòr's summit is a stiff climb, but the terrain is smooth.

Returning, I found the often-elusive east-west ledge that supposedly eases the ascents and descents – I have mentioned it in past articles – but think it not worth the bother. However one goes, one must climb 2,000 feet and there are no elevators. You wouldn't want them, for the climb is the fun. And the challenge.

Na Creagan is located at NGR NF 790 360. Otherwise, all relevant map references are provided after previous articles.

35. *Liathdail, Sheileasdail*

Glen Liathdail

THIS article will be different from my others. Usually I write about walks that I have already taken. Instead, I shall describe a walk that I haven't taken yet, but mean to take on my forthcoming summer visit – indeed, may have taken by the time the current (August) issue hits the shops, if my plane lands safely on 28 July and the weather and my legs hold up.

I have seen Glens Liathdail (Liaddale) and Sheileasdail (Hellisdale) before: gazed down upon them from the tops of Beinn Mhòr and Beinn Corradail (Ben Mòr and Ben

Corrodale); even passed through them en route to Gleann Corradail (Glen Corrodale) via the gamekeeper's track or Bealach Crosgard (Crosgard Pass). Yet I have never really explored them. I mean this time to do so.

There are many ways to reach these remote eastern glens, but the shortest and easiest – relatively speaking – is over Crosgard, the pass that separates Beinn Mhòr from its south-eastern neighbour Beinn nan Caorach (Hill of the Sheep). And there are many ways to reach Crosgard, but the shortest and easiest – again, relatively speaking – is the one I described in the last article. From the turn-about at the end of the North Loch Aineort (Locheynort) Road, take the public footpath through the 'forest': a worthwhile, if less ambitious, destination in its own right. Enjoy the vistas over Loch Aineort once the forest ends – they're best seen from the stone bench – and don't overlook the ruined customs house and inn, where galleys docked in the distant days when Loch Aineort was the island's principal port of entry.

Leave the path after the footbridge and proceed north over open country, circling approximately 180 degrees around the eastern shore of Loch nam Faoileann (Loch of the Gulls), and continue north past a deer fence – it will be on your left – to Crosgard's base, some two miles from your starting point. The terrain so far will have been fairly level, but you will have to scramble up a steep ascent to reach the pass.

From there you have choices. You can veer left and negotiate a longer, steeper ascent to the peak of 2,000-foot-high Beinn Mhòr. Or you can carry on straight into Liathdail and thereafter go across or around Maoladh nam Feannag (Mull of the Crows) into Sheileasdail. I've often done the former. For once I shall carry on.

The cliffs on the far side of Beinn Mhòr are a daunting spectacle when viewed from aloft. They must be equally so from below, though never having examined them closely from that direction, I shall have to reserve judgement. One approaches them by walking west around the southern shore of Loch Sheileasdail. I haven't done that either, but I'll do it in August and report back. There are also some interesting and well-preserved abandoned cottages at the northern edge of Gleann Sheileasdail, just below the forbidding Cas fo Deas (South Leg), which looms between Sheileasdail and Gleann Corradail. I have visited those before, on my way into Corradail, and look forward to seeing them again.

If you follow suit, a cautionary note: keep assessing your position in relation to clear landmarks – Beinn Mhòr, Rubha Sheileasdail (Hellisdale Peninsula) and of course the Minch. On my first trek into Corradail, fifteen years ago, I didn't, and wound up returning by helicopter: an experience that I have memorialized in several of these columns, and which I should like to forget, except that the locals won't let me. Small blame to them: it was their sleep I disrupted when the roaring bird circled and hovered in quest of me at 2 am.

Speaking of helicopter avoidance: now that we are in the midst of the hiking season, here are some tips for first-timers.

First: carry a walking stick. It's useful for balance, for crossing streams, for testing the depth of bogs, and above all for identifying what – if anything – lurks beneath the tall heather in front of you. It can spare you a broken limb by alerting you to slippery patches or hidden crevices.

Second: keep your eyes on the ground when in motion. If you see a sight worth admiring (and you'll see plenty, wherever you venture), stop to savour it; don't try to take it in while you're on the go.

Third: use your ears as well as your eyes. If you think you hear water gurgling, believe it – and watch out for the sharp dip that the heather conceals.

Finally, check yourself for ticks afterwards. They're subtler than midges, but their ill-effects can be much longer lasting.

My older son didn't believe me when I cautioned him that walking here has its hazards. That was before I pulled him out of the bog. He believes me now.

Safe journey.

Gleann Liathdail (Glen Liaddale) is located, or at any rate is centered, at NGR NF 830 300, Gleann Sheileasdail (Glen Hellisdale) at NGR NF 830 310. Both glens, of course, extend for considerable distances beyond these points. Maoladh nam Feannag (Mull of the Crows) straddles NGR NF 830 midway between 300 and 310.

36. Hill-walking on South Uist – August 2010

A beach on the Monachs; Eabhal (Eaval), Burebhal (Burrival) and the Lis (Lees) are in the distance

I'M settled into my Locheynort cottage as I write this article, and will remain through most of August. I haven't walked much yet, because – as the author of a book on the subject – I've been involved with the recent Battle of Prestonpans tapestry display on Eriskay: hosting the presenters, and helping to put up and dismantle the exhibit. But I've broken loose on two occasions. Both were memorable.

On Thursday, July 29, the day before the tapestry arrived, I made my first-ever visit to the Monach Islands (also known as Heisgeir) via Lady Anne Boat Trips, owned and operated by Nick Ingledew. Alasdair MacEachen, who has introduced me to so many of the Uists' outlying isles – see my previous columns about St. Kilda, Wiay and Sunamul – organised the venture. He was accompanied, as on the St. Kilda expedition, by his mother Katie, his sister Angela, and his nephew Allan.

The Monachs, situated five to eleven miles from North Uist and Benbecula respectively, are in stark contrast to St. Kilda, for they are almost flat, with their highest point being perhaps twenty feet above sea level. Whereas St. Kilda is known for its tall cliffs, the Monachs are remarkable for their white sand beaches. What the two archipelagos have in common is that their former populations have quitted them, so that their surviving structures now form ghost communities.

Two of the structures on Ceann Ear (East Head), largest of the Monachs – the school and the mission house – have been rehabilitated as museums. The latter contains wall plaques that set forth the islands' history. And therein lies a tale. My fellow passengers included a man, travelling with his teenaged son, whose great-grandfather had lived on the Monachs until 1898, when he'd given up and migrated with three neighbouring families to Sollas on North Uist. One of the wall plaques referenced this event. In consequence, my companion was able not only to confirm the circumstances of his ancestor's departure, but also to identify and view the ancient family croft.

The tapestry safely dismantled and en route to Arisaig – my house-guests gone with it – I endeavoured the following Wednesday to fulfil an intention I'd announced in my August article: namely, to explore Glens Liathdail (Liaddale) and Sheileasdail (Hellisdale). I was only partly successful.

I set out as planned, via Bealach Crosgard (Crosgard Pass) between Bheinn Mhòr and Beinn nan Caorach: a more direct, dry and scenic route than the one from the main road. I have described this route before, but shall now provide additional detail. You take the public footpath at the end of the North Loch Aineort road, just past a footbridge with a distinctive guillotine-like feature that keeps out deer. Stop, look to your right, and savour the views across Loch Aineort. Then leave the path and strike out north over open country to Loch nan Faoileann.

Circle around the Loch's eastern and northern shores till you come to a stream that tumbles downhill alongside a sheep track. Follow the track to the bottom, where the stream turns sharply eastward and you must cross it. (There are natural stepping-stones.) Almost immediately you will cross, as well, a stile over a barbed wire fence. Again, stop, look to your right, and savour the views across Loch Aineort.

There will now be a deer enclosure in front of you and on your left. Keeping the enclosure to the left, head uphill to where it ends. The terrain thereafter will be mostly level and grassy till you approach the Pass. There will also be a sheep track to guide you. Trust it: sheep don't do rocket science, but are superb at getting from Points A to B.

The entrance to the Pass is nasty, with scree, tall ferns, thick heather, and a steep ascent. But the sheep knew their way, so I followed their footsteps upward, just to the left of another tumbling stream. I saw human footsteps too. The Pass, once attained, is gentle. This time stop, look back, and savour the views across Loch Aineort.

Another fifteen minutes and I was through the Pass, gazing down into Liathdail and the Minch from the edge – or as close as I dared come to the edge – of some forbiddingly high cliffs. (My acrophobia did not kick in till I scrambled down their eastern flank almost to sea level and peered back up at them.) I could see across Liathdail's low floor into Sheileasdale, and could probably have gotten there, for I'd plenty of daylight. But I didn't trust my legs, and remembered ominously that this was where I'd gotten lost fourteen years earlier. That was less likely now, when I know the landmarks. Taking no chances, however, I turned back.

The distance each way was two-and-a-quarter miles (two to the Pass, a quarter-mile beyond). My total walking time, round trip, was four-and-a-half hours.

As for Sheileasdale? I'll try again.

Please consult the map references that appear after article No. 35 ('Liathdail, Sheileasdail').

37. Hillwalking on South Uist: Gleann Sheileasdail

Glen Sheileasdail

I keep my promises to my readers. And to myself. In my September article, I confessed to having wimped out of continuing from Gleann Liathdail (Liaddale) into Gleann Sheileasdail (Hellisdale) because I didn't trust my legs to carry me that far. But I also vowed that I would try for Shealeasdail again. And, on the very next day, I did.

Instead of starting from the North Loch Aineort footpath as I had done when going to Liathdail – a route that would have brought me through, or around, Liathdail via Bealach

Crosgard (Crosgard Pass) – I set out, at 9.15 am, from the improved Mill Croft footpath, just off the A865. The distance was longer: four miles each way, rather than three. But I wanted a change of scenery.

The footpath runs for about two-thirds of a mile. After it ended, I followed a low eastward-extending ridge that shielded me from the wet ground on either side, till I neared Maola Breac (Speckled Hillock). To avoid unnecessary climbing, I circled left around the Maola instead of crossing over it. I was now in Gleann Doirchaidh (Dark Glen). From there, I continued southeast – more east than south – as if heading to Beinn Corrodail (Corodale).

But I had no designs upon Corrodail, at least not then; rather, my target was Bealach Sheileasdail (Hellisdale Pass), on Corradail's right. The walk, across gradually rising terrain, was smooth as Uist walks go, except for the usual hindrances: bogs, tall heather, and streams – some of them broad, others narrow but well hidden, so that I had to feel for them with my stick lest I plunge into them. And the flies. Flies do not respond to what is known, in criminal law, as general deterrence: the notion that if you whack enough of them the rest will get the idea and back off. I killed them by the scores, for they were slow, yet their fellows kept attacking. I could have worn a cap with netting on it, but find that these caps obstruct my vision, so I left mine at the cottage – and paid the price.

I reached the pass at 11.45, and descended into the glen. Another half-hour brought me down to sea level, about halfway to the shore of the Minch. I did not proceed as far as Loch Sheileasdale – as on the previous day, I distrusted my legs – but I could see it clearly in the distance. I could also see, on my right, the dramatic palisades beneath the summit of Beinn Mhòr: the tallest and steepest of their kind on these islands, as far as I am aware.

Gleann Sheileasdail is rugged: so rugged that neighbouring Gleann Coradail, known for its forbidding landscape, seems almost park-like in comparison. Besides the palisades, there are huge rock formations throughout the elevated areas to the west, and the Abhainn Sheileasdail (Hellisdale River), bisecting the glen west to east, tumbles downward over a succession of tiny waterfalls until it crashes into the loch. Though August is a relatively dry month, its flow was powerful.

Even in that remote glen, I saw footsteps everywhere. I wasn't surprised, for I've learned that if one is pursuing a sensible route, others will have been there first. I was outraged: how dare these interlopers invade my kingdom? Just kidding; if I felt that way, would I write these articles? Actually, I found the footsteps reassuring – they confirmed that my route was sensible – as mine may do for you.

I spent a quarter-hour exploring before turning back at 12.30. I exited over the pass at 1.05. As I did, I gazed wistfully north at Beinn Corrodail. A few years ago I would surely have climbed it, and I think I could have climbed it that day, for its peak, I estimated, was only a half-hour away. But I'll either turn seventy shortly (about when this newspaper appears) or I won't, and I prefer the former alternative. So the watchword was caution. Besides, I wanted to see the Iochdar-Southend football match, which was to begin at 5 pm (it didn't – but I couldn't predict that), and a disconcerting dark cloud that had hovered all day seemed suddenly to be spreading (it ultimately passed harmlessly – but I couldn't predict that either). I therefore pressed determinedly onward, steeling myself not to look back until the hill was out of range, lest my resolve weaken.

As I rounded Maola Breac, I searched for the ridge that would lead me back to the path, but it was too low to spot at that distance. I eventually found an ATV track to the path. I returned to my car, which I'd left near the A865, at 3.35: three hours in, three out.

I'll describe other recent walks in the coming issue. I promise.

One circles around Maola Breac (Speckled Hillock) at NGR NF 790 340. Bealach Sheileasdail (Hellisdale Pass) is located between NGR NF 810 320 and NGR NF 820 320. Other relevant map references are provided after article No. 35 ('Liathdail, Sheileasdail') and previous articles.

38. Hill-walking on South Uist: Mhòr, Spin, Loch Aineort Paths

Stuleval and Arnaval from Spin

IT wasn't because I was being macho. It wasn't even because I wanted to show my older son Max's visiting girlfriend South Uist's finest panoramas. I just wanted to see whether I could still do it. And so, this past August, I climbed Beinn Mhòr twice: once alone and once with Max, Roxanne (the girlfriend), and Ben the ageless collie: film star, mountain guide, and treasured companion of my North Loch Aineort neighbours John Joseph and Isabel MacDonald.

I did both walks from the North Loch Aineort side, setting out from the public footpath at the end of the road and continuing along routes that I have described many times before. The first – by myself – was via Loch an Dorain. You begin by following the public footpath to, but not over, the footbridge. Then take the new footpath west to the three-tiered stile at the loch. Once over the stile, head north, straight towards the mountain, through a cut-away section of a barbed wire fence. Next, cross another footbridge, ahead and slightly left; it's easy to spot, for it bears a distinctive red circlet above its far post. From there, turn towards Mhòr once more, carry on across the gamekeeper's ATV track to its base, and start your ascent.

About halfway up, you'll reach a ledge. I've wavered, in past articles, as to the ledge's precise location, but I think I can now pinpoint it: it's an extension of Bealach Spin (Pass of Spin), which connects Mhòr to the hill of Spin, Mhòr's smaller, but still formidable, western neighbour. Keep that in mind, and you'll spot it even from afar. Walk east along the ledge till you come to a point directly below where the crest starts to dip. Scramble up to the crest, which is further away than it looks. Once you've attained it, reverse direction and resume climbing, more or less northwest, past the easternmost of Mhòr's three cairns and finally to the middle cairn, which marks the summit. The zigzagging increases the distance but avoids some dauntingly steep ascents.

I stopped at the eastern cairn, because a cloud suddenly swept around from the west and enveloped me. Recalling a similar experience atop Stuleval, I was anxious to drop below it as soon as possible, so I felt my way downwards, cautiously, until I could see clearly again. It had taken me three hours to get to the cairn, but I'd dawdled some, exploring the vicinity of the ledge. The journey home, in contrast, took only an hour and fifty minutes. A supper invitation awaited me, and, not wishing to be late, I descended perhaps more rapidly than was prudent.

When I returned with Max, Roxanne and Ben a few days later, we approached from a different direction. Leaving the public footpath only after we'd crossed the bridge, we veered northeast towards Crosgard Pass between Mhòr and Beinn nan Caorach (Hill of the Sheep). This route brought us around the eastern shore of Loch nam Faoileann (Loch of the Gulls) and past a deer fence, to our left, on rising ground. We'd planned on entering the Pass and climbing from there, but instead took advantage of some sheep tracks, immediately west of it, which provided a short cut to the crest. Even after we'd found the crest, it was still a good half hour to the nearest – that is, the eastern – cairn. Again we halted at that one, for the same reason: sudden, blinding cloud cover. Our walking time: about two-and-a-half hours each way.

Before Max, Roxanne and my wife came to the island, I attempted one other assault on Mhòr: on this occasion, from the water station off the A865. My destination was the northwestern cairn – the furthest of the three from Loch Aineort. The expedition had an unexpected though by no means unpleasant ending. I proceeded almost due east (tilting slightly south) across Beinn a Charra to Bealach Spin, a distance of just under two miles. Here I had an option: I could turn left, to Mhòr, or right, to Spin, which is 356 metres tall compared to Mhòr's 620. My heart yearned for Mhòr – I wanted to see whether I could still do it, remember – but one of those ominous rain clouds hovered above me. So I chose Spin, and made a welcome discovery: it took me only an hour-and-a-half to reach its summit compared to two hours from Loch Olaidh an Ear. The southern views, from that summit, were nearly as grand as from Mhòr itself.

Aside from these adventures, and from my solitary excursions into the eastern glens, which I recounted in the last two issues, I took most of my August walks closer to our cottage. I'll write about them next month.

One would cross Beinn a Charra from a point immediately northeast of NGR NF 770 320 to approximately NGR NF 780 320. Other map references appear after previous articles: Beinn Mhòr and the water station, after article No. 4 ('Hill-walking in June'); Crosgard Pass, after article No. 17 ('A Cautionary Tale'); Loch an Dorain and Loch nam Faoileann, after article No. 18 ('Beinn Mhòr in December')' Loch Olaidh an Ear after article No. 20 ('The Gamekeeper's track to Corodale'); and Spin and Beinn nan Caorach after article No. 29 ('Spin and Beinn Mhòr').

39. Hill-walking on South Uist – North Loch Aineort; Uisinis Point

North Aineort public footpath under snow, winter 2011.
Author at lower left

I reported the more ambitious rambles that I took this past August – to Leathdail, Shealeasdail, Mhòr and Spin – in my previous three articles. During the rest of my stay, I stuck close to our North Loch Aineort cottage, for I had guests who did not share my zest for hill-walking.

That's okay. There are plenty of worthwhile walks in our immediate area. And I did them: sometimes alone, sometimes with the guests, and sometimes with Beth, my wife – who likewise shuns the taller hills, but who enjoys the gentler excursions near the cottage.

I climbed Beinn Bheag Deas (Little South Hill) three times, including once with Beth. Since I've described this walk before, I'll skip over the details. The hill is relatively small - 167 metres – and one can reach the top, from the North Loch Aineort Road, in just 20 to 25 minutes. (I counted the paces, but somehow got inconsistent results: 1280 on one occasion, 1453 on another.) The ascent, however, is brisk; you get a workout. And the views from the top – east to Meall Mhòr; south across Loch Aineort; north to Beinn Mhòr above a valley with a half-dozen jeweled lochs – are stunning. Once on top, you can either retrace your steps back to the road, or you can keep going north, descend through a stile over a tall deer fence, and then, circling east, return via a new footpath.

This new footpath is the latest addition to an intricate skein of intersecting new footpaths that extend westward from the venerable public footpath at the North Loch Aineort Road's terminus. These paths provide so spectacular an introduction to the island that I show them to all of my guests; if they do nothing else, I tell them – if the weather, or their own more sedentary inclinations, keep them house- or hotel- or car-bound otherwise – they must do this. And the guests, even the ones least given to vigorous exercise, have relished the experience.

I've recommended the paths in past articles, but the new addition provides an even more attractive option. Take the public path to a footbridge that has a swinging barrier overhead to keep out deer. You'll pass other paths on your way, both left and right; ignore them. When you reach the footbridge, don't cross it; instead, turn left and follow a narrow path that runs parallel to a deer fence. This path will bring you to a three-tiered stile at the eastern edge of Loch an Dorain.

Hitherto I had advised readers next to double back and then swing right, at an intersection, onto another path that rejoins the public footpath closer to the road. No longer. Now you can carry on west, via the new extension. Get ready for two sharp left turns. The first, which is nigh-immediate, brings you about halfway up the north slope of Little South Hill; the second swings back east, along the slope, to the public footpath (after first connecting with the lower, right-hand footpath that I used to recommend). It's a stiff climb, but worth it, because you're high enough to see all of those jeweled lochs in the valley below Beinn Mhòr. How do you say 'wow!' in Gaelic?

There's a final treat. When you reach the public footpath, don't turn onto it; continue across it, on your present path, towards the coast. You'll pass a forest on your left. Search for a narrow tree tunnel, through the forest, that exits at a secluded rocky outcrop overlooking Bagh (Bay) Lathach. Take this short detour, and then return to the coastal path. It leads you back to the public path — I said that they all intersect — and thence to the road. Depending upon your pace, the entire outing should take from 45 minutes to an hour.

On a different subject: I've realized, after reviewing past columns, that I've never written about Uisinis (Usinish) Point on the east coast, site of the famous Stevenson lighthouse. For completeness's sake, I shall do so now, although I warn the reader that I went there only once, eleven years ago, and my memory of the specifics is hazy. Follow the Sgiopoirt (Skipport) footpath off the Sgiopoirt Road almost to the end, turn right through a (somewhat boggy) defile, and proceed in a southeasterly direction around Beinn na h-Aire. Shun the low ground to the east; it's wet. You'll see the lighthouse at the far end of a peninsula; there's a track as you approach it. It's about four miles each way, across wild, rugged terrain; bears would like it, if South Uist had bears. I'll go back some day. That's another promise.

Author's Postscript: Since this article was written, the new Loch Aineort footpaths have been extended further and it may take some trial and error to find the right ones. A caution: the highest path, directly beneath the stile, dead ends at its eastern extremity.

The Uisinish Point lighthouse is located about halfway between NGR NF 870 350 and NGR NF 880 350. The map references for Beinn Bheag Deas appear at the end of article No. 31 ('March Meanderings'). The map references for Loch an Dorain appear at the end of article No. 18 ('Beinn Mhòr In December').